Work on a Super Yacht

The Beginners Guide

Work on a Super Yacht

The Beginners Guide

Ben Proctor

Copyright © 2015 Ben Proctor

Amazon Edition

"This is a brilliant book ... Would recommend this as a must buy for anyone wanting to go into the industry." Written by "Mick" on 5 January 2014

"Accurate, informative, honest, and gold dust for anyone wanting to get into the industry. What Ben has produced will save you hundreds of euros and hours of time. Apply what's written and it will give you your best chance. Buy it! Everything you need" iBooks review March 2013

"Brilliantly Useful. Fantastic for anyone looking into a career on a super yacht! I will personally be using much of this book to pursue my next job!" Written by "Chris" on 21 May 2014

"Fantastic guide, full of practical advice. Excellent guide for getting started in the industry. Well written. Extremely useful. Would definitely recommend to anyone interested in such a career." Written by "Cooker" on 5 April 2013

Work on a Super Yacht

The Beginners Guide

About the Author : Prologue : The Super-Yacht
Industry : Super-Yacht Seasons : Working on a
Super-Yacht : Day in the Life : Living Conditions On-
board : Jobs on a Super-Yacht : Essential Courses
and Qualifications : The Super-Yacht CV : How to
Secure that Dream Job : Final Thought : Personal
Accounts of Working on a Super Yacht : Glossary :
Appendix : Useful Websites and Links : Sample CV :
Acknowledgements

About the Author

I started yachting aged twenty eight. Prior to this I was in a successful job earning an above average salary but deep down I was not content. My work in an office was mundane, and although it was Monday to Friday, nine to five, it lacked excitement, change of routine or dynamism. I realised I was stuck in a rut and no longer living life to the full. Alongside this I had an uneasy feeling that I was not ready to settle down; there was still more exploring left in me. I had thought about time out to consider career options, but having had two of these already I knew I would be no further forward and would just end up deeper in debt.

It was around the time of my third early mid-life crisis (!) that a friend of mine had started work on a Super Yacht. He was one of those people who fill their Facebook with amazing photos and exciting newsfeeds which can be highly depressing when you are living a more mundane existence.

I happened to bump into this friend when he was on leave and the normal chat started about life and how things were going. I'd regaled my news within 20 seconds; it is surprisingly difficult to make an office job sound exciting. However I was soon listening to stories about the Super Yacht world, of celebrities staying on board, visiting beautiful places in the Mediterranean and Caribbean, water sports galore and numerous exciting stories. To my surprise he informed me that his earnings were £2000 tax free a month and on top of this, from June to September, he received tips from guests in excess of £18,000! The thought of the travel coupled with the earning potential to establish some financial stability, sowed a massive seed in my mind. It would give me the opportunity of time out to explore working in the yachting world and time to consider other career options.

Despite being very excited by the thought of this adventure, my sensible side, that little voice in my head that I never quite know is Mr Reason or Mr Boring was saying, "don't leave your secure job for an industry you are new to. Stay at home in your comfortable flat, appreciate the security and your monthly pay check ..... Why take the risk?"

The months went by. Mr Boring ruled my head, though the seeds had been sown. I began sharing my friend's yachting experiences and my thoughts with family and friend's. Everyone seemed to think I was crazy to stay in a job I was not enjoying when I had absolutely no commitments. I was single, (not for want of trying) but unfortunately Cheryl Cole was just not looking for a 9-5 office worker. To add to that I had no mortgage and no dependents. With this in mind I decided to take a trip to the South of France to look at these yachts and see whether I should enter this industry or put the idea to rest once and for all. Could I persuade the Mr Boring in my head for once to take a chance on the journey that would change my present and maybe future life forever?

I spent a week in France staying in a beautiful town called Antibes. I left Nice Airport at 1030am on the return journey, arrived in Bristol at midday and was straight into work. By 1430pm I had handed in my notice, and my journey was about to begin......

Prologue:

The purpose of writing this guide is to share all I learnt from my experience. I was fortunate to have a friend in the industry who gave me many pointers, but I also had to do a tremendous amount of research and learn for myself through trial and error. I am continually receiving emails from friends, and friends of friends, asking for information and advice on working in the industry and I realised there was a strong need for a guide to help those considering work in the super yacht world.

I hope this guide will help. It is a totally honest account, and I make no apologies for any negative comments that may come across. I have endeavoured to be as honest as possible to enable the reader to make an informed decision based on all the facts.

This guide is aimed at anyone considering entering into the super yacht industry; increasing their knowledge in this highly competitive arena. It is an honest account from someone who has worked within the industry and learnt the realities first hand; both the good and the not so good. It is full of pointers and tips to help get started. A useful selection of essential website links are enclosed to strengthen your knowledge, as well as some technical terms. It is also aimed to help the reader learn how to stand out from the crowd and assist on the quest to achieve that dream job

If I can achieve my goal of working on a super yacht, then so can you. I hope this guide is informative, insightful and that it provides a greater understanding and knowledge.

I hope your journey is as exciting as mine has been with lots of happy times, personal development and memories to last a lifetime.

So let our journey in the world of Super Yachts begin.

The Super Yacht Industry:

Coming from the UK and growing up in Cornwall, I would previously have described a super yacht as a sixty foot Sunseeker motor boat. However a super yacht makes this type of boat seem small fry. There is one that has a sixty seven foot Sunseeker just as its tender (Le Grand Bleu).

A super yacht by definition is a pleasure yacht in excess of 24 meters in length. My definition would be, "an obscenely large yacht, the size of which can be difficult to comprehend. It is a structure that is immaculately maintained, providing a six star level service and one of the absolute epitomes of stature money can buy."

Superyachts are the absolute height of luxury and although the industry was affected by the recent recession in respect to crew jobs and wages, the number of yachts owned seems to keep growing, with new ones continually coming out of the ship yards.

Currently the largest operational super yacht is 'Motor Yacht Azzam', which knocked Mr Abramovich's yacht 'Eclipse' off the top spot in April 2013. Its overall length is 180 meters, requiring a rumoured eighty strong crew. Speculations as to its actual cost are rife, but figures around £400 million have been documented. Eclipse, the former largest super yacht, is said to accommodate some thirty guests in fifteen cabins, with a 16m swimming pool and a three-person leisure submarine. It is also said to house three helicopters. There is a great deal of secrecy surrounding many of these yachts, making them so valuable to their owners. The yacht is their haven of peace and privacy, as well as a symbol of wealth and status.

Currently the top 100 superyachts in the world range from 180 to 75.75 meters. The running costs vary but it is estimated that it is approximately 10-15% of the original price of the yacht; e.g. a yacht just over 60 meters (purchase price around £60 million) would cost around £5-6 million per year to keep operational.

Super yachts have different itineraries depending on the owners' requests. The majority from April to early October will be in the Mediterranean, making this an ideal time and place to look for work. Some will remain in the Mediterranean for the UK winter either in dock or in a shipyard for maintenance work. Others will head to the Caribbean, America (Fort Lauderdale in Florida) or increasingly popular destinations are the Pacific and Indian Oceans. A small minority may be involved in around-the-world trips heading anywhere…even to Antarctica.

Super Yacht Seasons:

Below is a brief summary of the typical yacht seasons to help you understand a general over view of yacht itineraries.

Mediterranean Season

-   Runs from April to October

-   Main places for work Antibes, Palma, Majorca and also other ports along the south coast including Monaco and Cannes.

-   Crew start looking for work March/April time. By April Antibes will be busy with new crew looking for work

-   The Monaca Yacht Show runs at the end of September and is a good time to secure day work. At this time of year you may also secure a position for a Trans-Atlantic crossing.

Caribbean Season

-   Yachts head for the Caribbean from October onwards

-   The main docks for super yachts are Antigua and St Maarten where yachts will generally pick up guests and owners from.

-   The Antigua Yacht Show runs at the beginning of December and draws a large concentration of super yachts.

-   This season ends in April then most yachts head back to the Mediterranean. Yachts will often stop in ship yards before the start of the Mediterranean season.

The States

- Some yachts may head directly to the States instead of the Caribbean from October onwards, while some will head to the States during the Caribbean season.

- The Fort Lauderdale International Yacht Show runs at the end of October to early November which draws some yachts.

- Generally yachts head to the East Coast to places like Florida or even New York.

- Some yachts will venture to the West Coast or even venture up to Alaska

The Pacific

- Where most yacht crew hope their yacht will take them! This is becoming more popular. Generally the yachts head here after the Caribbean season in March/April via the Panama Canal.

- The places that are visited could include Galapagos Islands, Pacific Islands (Tahiti, Fiji, Tonga) around May – September. Then onto New Zealand and Australia in November – May.

Types of Super Yacht

There are two main types of super yacht – motor and sail.

Generally the work on sailing yachts (or Wind Faggots as nicknamed by the motor yacht fraternity) will be more hands-on for crew with the actual sailing of the yacht. These yachts tend to employ crew with good sailing experience.

The motor yachts are nicknamed Stink Pots by the sailing world, an apt name due to their exhaust fumes.

As a very general rule, motor yachts tend to have larger crew living areas, they often employ more crew which can offer better opportunities to find people you get on with and generally tend to pay more. The work on these involves mainly cleaning and maintenance purely because they are generally larger with more surface area to clean and their fumes produce more dirt. As a very general summary what I tended to notice, and this is not true for all yachts, was that motor yachts tend to run a more regimented routine on board whereas those that sail have a more laid back attitude. Those with more limited boating experience are more likely to find work on a motor yacht.

Sailing yachts tend to have a more varied schedule, you may take part in super yacht cups and regattas and enjoy some great sailing experiences. It is likely that on a sail yacht you will be working in closer proximity to your crew and guests, mainly because their deck and interior is smaller than that of a motor boat. The crew on a sailing yachts tend to receive lower salaries compared to motor yacht crew and often do their job for their passion of sailing.

The yachts will generally be used for private use or charter, or a combination of the two.

Private yachts are used solely by the owner. Monthly wages are usually slightly higher compared to a charter yacht, commanding up to an additional 500 euros a month more for junior crew. It is less likely that the owner will tip, although some do.

Charter yachts are rented out to paying guests (charter clients or guests) who pay large sums of money to hire. It can cost up to one million euros a week. The fee only includes the hiring of the yacht and crew. It does not include food, wine, fuel, crew tips, or berthing fees (berthing alone can cost up to 2,000 euro a night). To cover these costs there is an additional fee, normally around a 10-15% of the charter fee and there is an expected (but at the guests discretion) 10-15% crew tip.

Though these yachts are chartered the owner may still use them for their personal use at allocated times through the year. One I worked on was only used by the owner twice a year. These dates were pre booked a year ahead and for the remaining time it was available for charters.

Normally significantly more can be earned on a charter yacht because of the crew tips. For this reason it can be harder to get work on these due to the volume of applicants, especially if new to the industry.

Yachts are becoming ever more sophisticated and larger in design and the industry is without doubt growing at a rapid pace. Alongside this the industry is becoming much more regulated and in some respects even more professional. With this comes much more paperwork for the more senior crew members. While this increased regulation can be seen as negative to more senior crew it does mean a greater attention is paid to the safety aspects on board, which has to be a good for the crew, owners and charter guests.

Working on a Super Yacht

As I said at the start, I hope this will be an honest portrayal showing the positive and negative aspects of the industry. I feel sure if the reader were to look through my Facebook pages you would leave your current job and head into yachting straight away! My photographs portray the very good side of yachting and there certainly is a great side to it; beautiful locations, lovely weather, water-sports and socialising. There is however another side which I will outline in this chapter.

Working on a super-yacht can, to some extent, be likened to working in a luxurious hotel. The difference being that the yacht is not only the place of work but also home, with less space than the average hotel, and of course always on the sea.

The level of service and maintenance has to be of the highest standard which is why the industry is often described as providing a six star level of service. These yachts have to be at the top of their game. Anyone paying up to 120,000 euros a night would expect something pretty fabulous. With this goes an insane attention to detail, so those who hate being incredibly thorough are going to find it very hard, as I certainly did at the start.

The industry has also become highly popular, and with this comes increased competition when trying to land that first job. This increase in popularity and in the regulations imposed, especially with the larger yachts, has meant qualifications are a must. Several years ago searching for a job without formal qualifications and through contacts was feasible. Certain qualifications are now a must and landing a position within a few days of stepping off the plane is unlikely but does happen. So the reality is that training is essential prior to looking for work, costing around £1000. The time in finding employment can vary greatly depending on qualifications, quality of the CV, competition, demand for jobs and how proactive you are.

However it would be worth anticipating that it may take up to two months or more before landing a permanent post.

The workload on a super yacht varies incredibly. The busiest times are in the preparation for guests' arrival, when guests are on-board and preparing for a boat show or photo shoot. During a busy period, between twelve to eighteen hour days are quite common. While guests are on-board, a seven day week with no days off is worked, even if on-board for months. Our crew worked a twelve to fourteen hour shift system.

The larger yachts (over 60 meters) generally tend to have stricter shift systems than the smaller ones (less than 40 meters). The crew on smaller yachts may end up performing a variety of roles. They may for example be employed as a deck hand to work outside on the decks but be expected to help in the interior when deck duties are minimal, such as in port. Each yacht is different and the demands can change with each guest on board.

If you are a very independent person and resent people telling you where and when you are working you may find this hard, although it is something that I found easier with time. It is important to realise that you will have to do what is asked and that the guests will take priority over crew working hours.

For our last Mediterranean season we had ten weeks of charters, one for six weeks and two for two weeks. From June until the end of September I had only five days off. This was more than some crew, who had just a couple of days, while some had no time off at all. As a team member this means that for the majority of that time you will be working on-board with your fellow crew. The term cabin fever really does start ringing true at these times. Whilst I am a sociable person, I do enjoy time to myself and prior to yachting I needed lots of this time. Through this experience I have become better at sharing my time with others. I believe all crew members go through times when they really want to be on their own, but manage to find their own space, normally their bed or cabin. The other hard reality is that plans can change at the last minute. The weekend you have been looking forward to with special plans may have to be cancelled at the last minute because the weather or yacht plans change. You are informed that the weekend is a working weekend, no arguing or discussion. This is yachting and this is normal.

Daily Diary

I have provided a brief summary of an average day with guests on board to give a very rough overview of a day for a deck hand.

0345: Wake up to alarm from a very deep sleep. This for me is one of the worse parts of the day, leaving my warm bed, (narrower than a single bed) knowing my day starts here. This is when I question why I ever left work at home starting at 9am and giving me every weekend off. I peel myself out of bed and straight into uniform. I opt not to have a shower in the morning as it gives me an extra 15 minutes in bed. I shower and shave the previous evening. Men (and maybe some hairy women!) have to be clean shaven each day when are guests on-board.

0355: I wolf down a cereal bar and head onto deck, collecting my radio (the means to communicate on-board). I radio my crew mate who is on the 0000-0400 shift to relieve him from his duties. The yacht has shifts covering 24 hours a day, seven days a week whilst guests are on board. At this stage I am envious of my crew mate; he is now off to bed and has an eight hour break. He discusses what is left to do on deck, and I take over.

0400 – 0600: The majority of the guests have returned from their evenings out, so the passerale (the walkway connecting the yacht to the dock) is raised when the last tender run is completed. (Tender runs involve ferrying guests from the yacht to wherever they wish to go). Provided all guests are on-board the yacht will be cleaned as needed. The teak decks sometimes need a rinse but often a scrub is needed with cleaning products to remove any stains from food or salt water. It may also involve emptying and cleaning the Jacuzzi. I could also be involved in preparing the water sports room for activities that day as well as re-stocking the cooler bags with drinks and replenishing the towels outside. The whole yacht may need to be rinsed to wash away salt spray from the previous days cruising and dried with a shammy, although hopefully my crew mate on the night shift will have done this.

The tenders have to be cleaned also. The time goes quickly. I am working on my own and as there are normally no guests around, this is the time to do the jobs that cannot be done when they are present.

0600-0730: My work colleague joins me at 0600; starting his shift which will run until 2200 hours. He helps me finish any outstanding work and we then prepare for the guests once they wake. All outside seating areas would have been covered when guests retired to prevent dew or rain damaging the cushions. Once the sun has risen we uncover the seating areas, lay out sun loungers, lay tables with magazines, sun cream, fresh water and tissues on them. We place towels rolled neatly on the chairs and loungers. The drains running around the deck are cleaned with a mop, the stainless steel is buffed with a cloth and cleaning products and all tables wiped down and polished. If the yacht had not been rinsed overnight we wipe down all the flat surfaces with a damp shammy to remove any dust or hair that has collected on these surfaces. We aim to have everything set up and cleaned to an immaculate standard before the first guest wakes. It looks unprofessional to have water everywhere and crew carrying cleaning equipment while the guests are eating breakfast and reading their morning paper.

0730-0930: The guests often slowly start rising and the bulk of the work is now complete. We may be putting equipment away from their view or preparing to leave the dock.

0930-1200: Around this time we will often be leaving the dock so all lines will be brought on board and tidied away, fenders deflated and fender hooks put away. This keeps the main deck area tidy should guests come down, and erases any evidence of having been moored. Whilst the yacht makes its way to the days destination, we prepare for water sports activities and change into water-sports gear. As we approach our destination for the day we drop anchor. We then set up the swim platform with all the equipment, ringos, banana, slide, wakeboards, water-skis, jet skis and launch both tenders which are placed on whips off the side of the yacht. The swim ladder is also put in place and the bumpers slotted in. We keep at least one crew member on the swim platform at all times in case a guest comes down to swim or to use the equipment. Roughly every 30 minutes through the day the deck crew will carry out checks to ensure that all the exterior decks are tidy. This involves clearing glasses, towels, straightening cushions, topping up the jacuzzi, polishing finger marks off the stainless steel or cleaning the teak decks.

1200-1600: I am off duty though not a guaranteed if guests want to do water sports. If I do manage I will eat a quick lunch then go to my room/bunk and watch a DVD, read or sleep.

1600-2000: On-going water sports until the sun sets or guests have tired. All the water sports equipment has to be brought back, rinsed and deflated. The jet skis and tenders are also lifted on board and cleaned and the engines flushed with water. The swim platform is packed away, whips put away and the lazarette (water-sports garage at the back of the yacht) tidied. The anchors are lifted and we are underway to our next destination. On the journey I try to take a very quick shower, change into evening uniform (long trousers and shirt) and have a bite to eat. It is then time to prepare the lines, blow up the fenders and put in place ready for docking when all the deck crew are needed. I may not get to bed until 2000 hours though this has been closer to 2200 hours. I will be unlikely to get this time back and will lose sleep.

Once docked we organise a rota for passerale watch. This involves standing on the dock or yacht ensuring no undesirables enter, and keeping a tally of any guest leaving or returning. When my shift has ended I ask permission from my senior crew to retire to bed, normally around 2000 hours, ready to begin again at 0400 hours the following morning.

So it can be seen that a normal 12 hour day could easily creep up to 18 hours. This is not too frequent, and anything from 12 to 16 hours is commonplace.

The stewardesses/stewards work very similar hours. They are responsible for serving drinks and food as well as cleaning the living areas, guest cabins and shower rooms. Each time a guest has a shower it has to be cleaned. Bedding is changed a minimum of every other day, if not every day. They also lay and clear tables and wash dishes. When guests are using the water sports equipment, the stewards/stewardesses clean their cabins and when finished are on service for food or drink. They work hard with little time for breaks and have to remain on duty until all guests are in their cabins at night, and then remain on call. Therefore if there is a partying group they will often not get to sleep until the early hours, sometimes 6am. Like the deck crew, normal hours would be 12 to 16 and occasionally 18 hours.

During these long hours meal times for crew may be rushed or, as happens frequently, interrupted by a radio call for extra help or pick up guests in the tender.

Day work while on charter can vary hugely. Some days the guests may request a trip and on these occasions one or two crew may accompany them. The remaining crew will stay on board to maintain the cleanliness of the yacht. Other guests may be happy to sit at anchor in a location of their choice, and work is therefore much easier for the deck crew. However the stewards/stewardesses continue to have a large workload maintaining the cabins and service.

There are serious changes gradually being implemented as a result of the Maritime Labour Convention 2006, which aims to set out the rights of crew working on boats. One area covered is the rest time for crew hopefully having a positive impact on working hours. How effectively it will be implemented and the realities of how it will work will become more apparent with time. (For information on the Maritime Labour Convention 2006 follow the hyper-links within the appendix.)

When there are no guests and no preparations for any upcoming events the more civilised hours of 0800-1700 with an hour lunch break and two 15 minute breaks are worked.

Saturdays and Sundays are normally days off and occasionally a half day given on Fridays. Other yachts may be more generous with the Friday half day while some work different hours. Often in the Caribbean crew will work 0700-1300 hours. This is the time when crew are so very fortunate being moored in a glamorous location awaiting potential charters or the owners arrival. This is the time to see some incredible parts of the world. I was fortunate to spend weekends in the British Virgin Islands, Corsica, Malta, Antigua and St Maarten to name but a few.

Holidays from our yacht were not permitted when on standby for owners or a possible charter or on the Atlantic crossings (though the interior crew were generally allowed leave during these crossings). Holiday was permitted at the beginning or end of a season or during a shipyard period. Annual holiday entitlement varied from four weeks to six weeks. Crew working on a rotating rota may work two months on and two off or three, four and six month rotations. Rotations for junior crew are very rare and more common with senior staff e.g. captains, engineers, chief stewardesses/stewards, pursers and chief officers. Holidays are very yacht dependent and you would need to check the holiday policy of your specific yacht outlined in your contract. A private yacht that does not charter may offer greater flexibility with holiday as itineraries of guests may be known in advance, making allocation easier. However this is frequently not the case with guests turning up with minimal notice. The frustrating thing that I found with holiday planning was having to book everything at the last minute. It was hard with friends' weddings and special occasions as leave would often not be granted if the yacht was operational.

My normal leave was two weeks in May/June and two weeks in October. We were expected to work Christmas, New Year and Easter these being popular chartering times. I spent two Christmases working and always found this a very difficult time being away from family and friends and last year I vowed not to miss another one. For me this is a family time.

Living Conditions On Board:

It is usual to share a cabin; normally a narrow single bunk bed. Often there is only one cupboard, two if lucky and a small en-suite is shared consisting of a shower, toilet and basin. The cabins vary from two to three persons sharing and I have yet to hear of a four bedded one though am sure they exist. They are often small. Occasionally there is a desk but normally there is just a walk-way between the bunks to the en-suite. Generally the larger yachts tend to have larger crew areas though this varies and is dependent on the design specifications of the yacht. There is usually one crew mess but more on the larger yachts. These form the area for crew meetings, eating, socialising and watching television. The crew mess will often have fridges with drinks and cupboards containing snacks and cereals. They also often have built-in entertainment systems with numerous movies and music accessible via an Ipad. Most yachts provide all toiletries for crew. They also provide snacks which are freely available as well as fizzy drinks, fruit juices, beers and wine. I found these perks such a joy and became an expert in the best fragranced Lynx shower gels and whether the Gillette Mach 3 or Fusion razor was the best! Coupled with this, all food is provided by some of the best chefs. Our meals would regularly consist of steak, lamb, chicken, fresh fish, mussels, curries; and suffice to say I have never eaten such a diverse and high quality of food in my life. Adding these benefits to a monthly wage and taking into account that there is no spending on food, accommodation or toiletries, it is possible to save most of your monthly salary. My only expenses were entertainment in the evenings and weekends, i.e. a trip to the cinema, meals or drinks out. We also had access to cars hired for the yacht at each harbour (normally up to three for 16 crew) giving us freedom at weekends. So it can be seen that there are great bonuses and that crew are normally very well looked after.

However there are also sacrifices to be made living on board a yacht. All your personal habits will be known when sharing a cabin! There is limited personal space save your bunk bed and although the crew mess is a sociable area, it is often difficult to watch a film in peace without someone interrupting. Many captains run strict policies where only crew are allowed on the yacht, hence friends have to be met in bars. If in a relationship with a non-crew member, it may be necessary to meet at hotels for weekends.

Summary

Through being aware of both the positive and negative aspects of life on a super yacht you will not be going into the industry blinkered and I hope will have a more realistic outlook when you finally start.

Just remember that you will be at the service of the yacht and the yacht comes first in respect to your time and takes absolute priority, which can be difficult initially. I certainly found it difficult at the start having weekends cancelled and being so limited with holidays and time at home. It is also hard when working to get personal space and privacy. For me this intimacy only helps to stress an important point..... it is SO important you get on well with your crew. The crew are the most important part of a yacht, not how it looks or what it pays, and it is well worth getting it right.

 Is it right for me?

I have listed some of the important things to consider:

? You like boating/the sea

? You are sociable with people, like being around others and are happy to live in confined spaces and share a room with others.

? Enjoy working hard and sometimes partying hard

? Can cope with limited time at home with friends and family

? Don't mind your personal time and life being restricted

? Able to maintain a good outward happy persona even when tired

? Enjoy pulling together as part of a team to get a job done efficiently and to the best of your ability.

? Can cope with working long days and able to function with little sleep

? Are happy to clean things over and over again, even if may not appear overly dirty

? Happy to be told what to do, and do things even when you may not fully agree with them

? Happy to have your meals cooked for you and washing done for you!

? Enjoy providing a high level of service to wealthy clients

? Happy to have limited privacy in personal life (amazing what crews find out and how gossip spreads on-board).

? Happy to live on-board a superyacht and visit beautiful parts of the world

? Happy to swim in blue seas and sunbathe in hot weather all year around

…….. well maybe it is for you!

Joining the Yachting Industry and Where to Start?

If you have come this far and are still interested part of the hard work is done. I personally found making that decision quite a difficult one, but perhaps I do ere on caution.

Firstly consider which type of work suits you.

Deckhand:

Responsible for working as part of a team in the maintenance and management of the exterior of the yacht, including all exterior decks, the hull, tender garages, masts and basically everything outside. It also includes cupboards and storage spaces used by the deck department. The deck crew are responsible for all handling of lines when entering and leaving port and all anchoring procedures. They are responsible for safe tender driving, undertaking and teaching water sports. The vast majority of their time is spent outdoors.

Stewardess/Stewards:

Work as part of a team in the management of all interior accommodation areas in the yacht, to include communal crew as well as guest areas. The interior crew may assist the chef in the provision of food. They are responsible for excellent hospitality skills to guests on-board in the serving of drinks and food. They must also present the yacht to a very high standard, to include table decorations, and suitable colour scheming with dinner themes. The work is mainly based inside, which can be a bonus with air conditioning. The interior crew may also assist in laundry duties for crew and guests. However some yachts, especially larger ones, have laundry crew, responsible solely for all laundry.

Engineer:

This role is to maintain the smooth and efficient running of the mechanical elements on board. These include the engines, generators, sewage systems, water filtration systems, holding tanks and all electrical elements (from the entertainment system to changing a light bulb). Generally a considerable amount of time is spent in the engine room which may be a confined space and often hot, and involves oily and dirty work.

On the larger yachts it is becoming more common to see Electronic Technical Officers (ETO's). They are responsible, as the name suggests, for the electrical more technical side of engineering which could include the yachts on-board entertainment system, navigational equipment and communicational equipment.

Chef:

The chef is responsible for creating a broad and diverse range of meals for guests and crew. They are responsible for composing menus and ordering provisions of food for guests. Culinary experience is essential for the larger yachts, though smaller ones are often less strict on the level of skills required. This varies from yacht to yacht and is often decided by the captain and sometimes the owner. The number of chefs will vary depending on the yacht size

Other:

Other career options on yachts can include: Masseuse, Nurse, Beauty Therapist, Sports Therapist, Personal Trainer and Chiropodist. These roles tend to be on the larger yachts and job opportunities are more limited.

For further information on careers in yachting and career progression a well laid out website called SuperyachtUK is excellent for providing a wealth of information.

Visit:

http://www.superyachtuk.com/careers-1/job_descriptions.aspx

Relevant Courses, Qualifications and Certificates for the Industry

It is important to ensure the basic requirements expected are met before heading out in search of employment as this is such a competitive industry.

STCW 95: Standards of Training, Certification and Watch Keeping

This is the most important, and now an essential qualification and a legal requirement on boats over 24 meters. All super yachts now demand this qualification and you will not be considered without it.

The course costs around £850-£950 and is normally five days covering the following.

- First Aid

- Fire fighting (two to three days).A very thorough course using breathing apparatus, live fire scenarios and the use of hoses and extinguishers.

- Sea Survival

- Personal responsibility

There are numerous centres around the UK that run this course. Courses also run (in English) in Antibes in France and other locations around the world. An internet search engine will show the most appropriate course.

Other qualifications are optional, but I feel that with the current competition, these are certainly beneficial if not required.

Deck crew:

I would recommend undertaking a RYA Level 2 Powerboat course. For most yachts this is an essential qualification for driving the tenders, and shows a prospective employer that basic skills for tender driving has been achieved. Also of benefit is the PWC (Personal Watercraft) Instructors Qualification from the RYA. This is helpful as guests using the Jet ski's/PWC's will be required to have been instructed by a qualified instructor and given a licence prior to using a jet-ski on their own in certain areas. These courses will take at least a couple of days each but are certainly a very valuable asset on a CV.

Another qualification to consider for deck crew is the RYA Yacht Master Offshore qualification. This is an expensive course costing £800- £1000 if you have the required sea experience though more expensive if you need to build your sea hours through the course. This is an excellent and respected course that is detailed and is significantly more time intensive compared to the other qualifications. You will also need to have completed certain criteria prior to undertaking a Yachtmasters, see below link;

http://www.rya.org.uk/coursestraining/exams/Pages/Yachtmasteroffshore.aspx

The Yacht Master qualification is becoming more requested in the industry and to have this will certainly stand you in good stead. If I was to enter the industry now, I would strongly consider studying for this. It is also beneficial should you wish to make this a longer career option and be more knowledgeable during bridge watches and general procedures. It is a well-respected qualification in the industry and certainly worth serious consideration if you have the time and money.

Stewards/Stewardesses:

There are a host of steward/stewardess service courses to include Silver Service and many cookery and wine tasting courses that can boost your CV. These are available at most maritime training centres and found online. They are certainly valuable and add strength to a CV and confidence in competencies when starting work. Past work experience is of obvious benefit such as hotel, cleaning or bar work.

Engineering:

If considering this route it would be beneficial to have some engineering background or at least show this is an area of interest. It would also be advantageous to have completed your Approved Engine Course (AEC), costing under £1000.

ENG1 Medical

Anyone considering work on a yacht will require this certificate before going to sea. It is awarded on passing a basic medical performed by a registered Doctor and costs around £80. For a full list of approved doctors see http://www.dft.gov.uk/mca/mcga07-home/workingatsea/mcga-medicalcertandadvice/mcga-ml5-medicalinfo/mcga-approved-docs-list.htm)

The medical checks eye sight, hearing, colour-blindness and blood pressure. It can be carried out abroad if necessary but is much easier to organise before you leave. You are then ready to look for work on arrival, looking organised and committed to a potential employer.

The Super-Yacht Curriculum Vitae:

This should be no more than two sides of A4 paper and should include any relevant experience; i.e. work in hospitality or boating. Include anything that may be relevant to yachting as well as work experiences.

It is likely that your CV will improve as you meet agents and develop your experience on yachts, but it is advisable to have a sound basic outline before you leave the UK.

An outline CV is in the appendix as an example of the expected layout and style and it should include the following headings.

Name

Date of Birth

Phone Number: Include the local number of your whereabouts. If in France buy a local sim card and add the number to your CV, ensuring before you leave the UK that your phone will accept other countries sim cards or you can buy a cheap pay-as-you go phone abroad.

Address: Where you are staying.

Nationality and Visas: As per passport and any visas held.

Marital Status:

A photo: It is unusual to request a photograph for a CV, but for yachting it is expected. Whilst I would like to say looks are not a factor in yachting, I certainly feel there are some yachts that use looks as one of their main criteria for crew selection, although this tends to be more for the interior crew (especially stewardesses). The photo should be of you looking presentable and with a nice smile. They say "a picture paints a thousand words" so make yours happy, trustworthy and approachable and it will go a long way. In an industry that is so about appearance make sure your photo portrays this.

Smoking status: Non-smokers are more appealing to an employer and though most people have on their CV non-smoker it is amazing just many yacht crew smoke.

The Objective: Why you want to get into yachting and what are your plans in this industry? You need to make this appear a well thought out career plan, even if you are unsure how long it will be for. The pitch should show you are passionate and highly motivated for this career. You may want to use this section to outline your objective, for example "looking to develop my experience in yachting and sea time to apply for my Yacht Master in September 2013." This is your opportunity to tell the reader what work you are seeking, why you have chosen it and any future plans you may have.

Personal Statement: This is about you, what can you bring to the yacht and crew, and why you would be good for the position? Sell yourself in a positive way but try not to appear overly arrogant. You need to present yourself as someone who gets on well with others and is a great team player.

Qualifications and Experience: List any courses you have completed to include your STCW course and dates as well as any past work experiences relevant to yachting.

Employment History: Detail past employers with the most recent first. Keep as relevant as possible and brief. Include any hospitality experience, boating or previous yachting work. Include skills that may be useful in yachting and see if these can be tailored to experiences from previous work e.g. customer service, dealing with clients, cleaning and team work. Try to show as many transferable skills as possible keeping them relevant to yachting.

Hobbies and Interests: It is worth remembering that you will be sharing a cabin and living with others, so it is important to list hobbies to show you are well-rounded. Team sports are good showing you get on well with others and work well in a team, though any sport is good. Skiing/snowboarding are often popular past times among yacht crew and water sport skills are very desirable. Perhaps you can wakeboard, ski or learnt basic sailing skills at school?

References: Prior to departure ensure you have two suitable references. One should be your last employer. For the second a really good character reference will be well received.

It is also advisable to ask your references to provide a copy of the reference. I feel it is so much better give out your CV with two shining references stapled to the back. This will not only impress the Captain but will put your CV ahead of the vast majority and save him chasing references for you. Throughout my time in yachting I have seen a hundred CV's but not one included a copy of their references typed and stapled to the back and yet it is very easy to do.

A simple design looks good though it is an idea to do something to make it stand out. Keep the style clean and clear with a well laid-out design, subheadings and bullet points. Ensure it is easy for the reader to read without too much information.

Of note: Before I left the UK I printed forty CV's. However I would advise you only print off two in your first week when looking for work as each agent will tell you something different, to add or change. Also if you are successful in obtaining day work in your first week your CV will then need updating. I suggest you take a copy of your CV on a USB or your laptop, so you can edit and reprint it.

Business Cards:

This is optional. I printed, very cheaply online a basic business card outlining my name, qualifications, experience and the work I was looking for and attached this to my CV. Maybe no one ever even used this card but my aim was to create a professional look and stand out from the numerous CVs received that day.

You are now getting there, your qualifications completed, CV and references and maybe some business cards too.

CHECKLIST

To help with all your organising and planning:

> Decide on your departure date, giving a goal to aim for

> Complete STCW 95 course

> Organise further courses e.g. Powerboat level 2, personal watercraft instructor, silver service etc.

> Visit dentist and optician prior to having your ENG1 medical. It is much easier to sort things in your own country. Keep your prescription for glasses/contact lenses and take with you.

> Organise and attend ENG1 medical

> Book flight

> Book crew accommodation

> Write CV

> File your CV, references, qualifications and certificate in a plastic presentation folder. This will keep everything together and will look more professional

> Photocopy certificates, passport, driving licence, prescriptions etc. in case lost. Scan and email to your account to keep safe.

> Register with crew agencies (see later)

> Inform Tax office of departure (if from UK complete a P85 tax form and send.) I met many people who failed to inform the tax office of their plans, causing considerable hassle. (See end of article for download link for a P85 form.)

> Ensure all mail is redirected to a suitable location (I used my parents address)

> Email any contacts who have worked in the business as they may just have a contact that opens your first door in yachting.

> Create business cards online

> Contact referees

> Ensure you have a mobile phone that does not have a locked sim so you are able to add sim cards from other countries, making calling and texting cheaper with no cost to you when receiving calls from abroad.

> Look on websites such as Yachting Times and Charter Agent sites (links at end), to get an idea of yachts on the market. It is good to add to the excitement of your new venture as well as familiarising yourself with some. Register with Dockwise Magazine for free email updates with the latest information on what is happening in the industry, (link at end).

> Ensure you have sufficient supplies of medical and personal requirements.

> Consider taking a small diary to record events. It is helpful to keep a record of your sea time if you wish to develop your career.

> Ensure you have a laptop with WIFI as many yachts have WIFI access. I also had a DVD player on my laptop and a large external hard drive to store any movies. It is sometimes good to watch a DVD in your own space, and a real luxury when sharing so much time with others. I also downloaded Skype before I left which proved my main way of communicating with family. It was free and great to see them on the video link.

> Some crew set up off-shore accounts. I had my money transferred straight into my UK account and declared all my income to the tax office with an annual self-assessment, through an account specialising in Maritime Workers, (link at the end). For me this worked as I knew I wanted my money to

end in the UK, where I planned to return, and the exchange rates were good. However if you want an offshore account it does mean you can hold currency in, I believe, up to three currencies. I did not want the hassle and opted to use my UK current account and debit card which I could use anywhere to withdraw money. I met a mix of people who did as I did and others who had off shore accounts. Generally those in the industry for more than a year tended to have offshore accounts. I would suggest you speak with a local independent financial advisor if unsure. Note: If you have any questions with regards tax while abroad, speak with your local tax office. I declared all my income to the UK annually to keep the tax office informed.

> Contact your bank prior to your departure to inform them of any debit or credit cards you will be using abroad. This will stop them freezing your account when they notice abnormal spending activity abroad.

Securing that Job:

This is a very competitive market with considerable competition. However there are opportunities everywhere and situations can change within a minute. A crew member may be fired for poor behaviour or resign, so opportunities do come up. However you need to get yourself out there to make opportunities happen.

So how can you make this happen? I can only speak from my own personal experience and other peoples experiences and will endeavour to describe the four main ways of securing work.

Dock-walking:

This I found the most nerve wracking aspect of looking for work and it basically involves walking the docks and approaching the yacht's crew. The aim is to achieve any or all of the following; to leave a CV, to secure some day-work, secure a permanent position and/or to make the crew/captain aware of you and your availability for work. The good news is that most crew have experienced this daunting process so they understand how intimidating it can be and are therefore more than happy to help. It does get much easier with time, practice and experience. Ensure you are looking presentable, approach with a smile and be polite and courteous. It is surprising how far a smile goes to making a good impression to crew, and how the effect of a recommendation from a crew member can mark your CV above numerous others. It is often worth asking to speak to more senior staff about possible opportunities; this could be the 1st or 2nd Officer for deck crew or the Purser or Chief Stew for interior crew, the Head Chef for potential chefs/cooks and the Chief Engineer for Engineering. It is probably best not to request the Captain, they are busy people and to be disturbed for a dock walker will only go against you.

A good dock-walker is smart, apologises for disturbing you and introduces themself. They ask if there are any positions available or likely to be, politely ask if they can leave a CV, again apologise for disturbing you and thanks you for your time and wishes you a good season. This makes a significantly better impression than when crew find a CV tucked under the mat at the bottom of the passerale. As an absolute last resort leave a CV under the mat if no one is around but always follow this up by calling to the yacht the following day to confirm they received it.

I have met many people new to the industry looking for work who would say "dock walking is a waste of time; you never get jobs from dockwalking." I personally disagree. Ironically it is often these people who struggle to get work and spend most of their time in the pub. Dock walking is an excellent opportunity to sell yourself, build your confidence and make an impression on a potential employer. Dock –walking secured my first permanent position and I even had one yacht email me six months after asking if I wanted an interview for a permanent position.

I would always ensure I was on the dock by 0745 to catch the crew when they were first on deck and try to beat other dock-walkers. I would also attempt to do more than one port a day, e.g. I would walk Antibes in the morning, then get a train to another dock and return to dock-walk Antibes again in the afternoon. I would also do the same in Monaco, Nice, and Cannes once or twice a week. During peak season (May to early September) it is worth dock-walking every day including weekends. Outside peak season Monday to Friday is sufficient.

Crew Agents:

Crew agencies are basically recruitment agents that place crew on suitable yachts. Some say they are not useful for those new to the industry, but they seem to be having an ever stronger presence for placing new crew on yachts. I personally found a few who were most helpful and worked hard to find me work. Certainly it is true to say agencies have more use the more qualified and experienced in the industry you become. There is a list of the crew agencies at the end of this guide.

Crew agents use online systems requiring you to register online with them to create your "crew profile" to include your name, contact details, photo and CV. They may ask what you are looking for with regards work and your plans. Registering can be time consuming so it is best to register with them before leaving. Once abroad it is advisable to meet the agents. Remember they meet numerous people in the same situation so you need to make a good impression. They are looking for someone who is reliable, smart, cheerful and committed. Turning up hung-over, non-shaven and looking dishevelled will certainly make the wrong impression.

You should aim to make contact with your agent at least once a week to let them know what you have been doing, and meet face to face. I kept in touch with all my agents, but had two I favoured and called in to see personally, phoned, or as a last resort emailed on my progress. I also logged onto their website most days as with most of the agencies online systems each time you log on it shows you are still looking for work. The nearer you are to the top of their list shows you are an active member looking for work.

Socialising:

This is a very social industry and meeting people is a good way of finding work and making new contacts. This may include staying in a crew house or meeting people in a bar. Remember this is a relatively small industry so try to make a good impression with all you meet and take the opportunity to socialise with as many crew as possible. Beware not to look too much of an alcoholic as this can have a negative effect as it did for some I lived with. Popular bars in Antibes often full with crew during the summer are The Hop Store, The Blue Lady and The Drinkers Club.

It is also worth asking friends at home if they know anyone in the industry as this can be a good link and may provide an opportunity. It is surprising where an opportunity may present itself. Keep social, use any contacts you may have and look to meet new people.

Day working:

This is often the end result of any of the previous three options and is a way into a job. Most yachts will start you working on a daily basis offering around 100-120 euros a day. This is how most people looking for work fund their search while gaining valuable experience for their CV. Day working often involves the less glamorous jobs; to include cleaning engine rooms, storage tanks and cleaning outside.

This is an excellent opportunity to sell yourself and make a good impression, so it is advisable to work hard and be polite. Often there may be the chance of a permanent position though the yacht may not inform you until they are happy with you and your work ethos. The yacht I worked on told me there were no positions available and after two weeks of day work I was a full time crew member!

It is very easy to spot a good worker even if they have little yachting knowledge. They complete a task even if it runs into the end of the day, are not asking for their break and you may even have to tell them to stop working. I was once working with another day-worker who was very chatty, funny and appeared to get on well with the crew. I felt sure the crew would pick him over me should there be a job available. However I found out later that the crew felt he was too confident at this stage in his career, did not work as hard as me and his chatting actually irritated them. I was delighted and surprised to be offered the post.

It is worth remembering that often there is CCTV on-board. I know one chap who gained a job not only from crew recommendation but also from his hard work viewed by the Captain on CCTV.

When and Where to Look for Work?

The time I would recommend, and recommended by crew agents, is to head to the South of France from March to April, when the yachts are getting ready for the Mediterranean season. This is the busiest season for the majority and when most jobs are available. It is also the time when most people are actively seeking work, especially new deckhands and stewardesses.

Also consider the south of France towards the end of the Mediterranean season from August to September. My personal feeling is it can be risky as many yachts will stay in the Mediterranean and reduce crew numbers, so you will be competing with others who have been working since the start of the season with more experience. Having said this I ventured out on 3rd September very motivated to look for work each day. I found there were certainly opportunities with crew leaving having made good money that season to return home or maybe do a ski season. It is also possible to find work with yachts in shipyards, as often crew will choose a more exotic location than a shipyard to spend their winter. Although the shipyards are not the most glamorous aspect of yachting they are an excellent grounding for someone new to the industry, especially those looking to join the deck or engineering departments. La Ciotat in France is a busy ship yard at the beginning and end of the season as well as during the winter, so it is often a good place to look for day work. The Monaco Yacht Show takes place in September and is also recommended for day work and job opportunities, which often become available through agents. The Mediterranean season seems to get much quieter two weeks after the show as yachts leave for shipyards, layups for the winter or the Caribbean or Pacific.

My recommendation would be to go to Antibes in the South of France. The nearest airport is Nice with regular flights from most UK airports and a popular destination with British

Airways and Easy Jet. As France is in the European Union there is no problem with Visas.

Antibes has fantastic access to crew accommodation, crew agents as well as a great variety of docks to walk with easy commute times. These include Cannes, Nice, Monaco, Juan Les Pins, La Ciotat (ship yard) and other smaller ports. The South of France offers the best access to these yachts. The dock security, if present, will allow you access for dock walking. The South of France also supports the four main ways of looking for work outlined previously.

Due to the popularity of Antibes I would recommend booking crew accommodation before you leave as they are often fully booked from April to September.

Crew accommodation is basically a professional youth hostel, rooms of two to six people, with communal showers, toilets, kitchen and living areas. They often have computers, WIFI and printers (for printing out the numerous changes you'll be making to your CV!)

My recommendations would be the Crew Grapevine. I stayed here and found the owners and staff very helpful and friendly. Other crew recommend the Glamorgan, (links at end). These crew houses are social, receive day work opportunities and are a good place for networking. There are cheaper ones so it is worth looking online to see what suits you and your budget. Having had a gap year, and as a more mature person entering the industry I wanted a pleasant place to stay, not a return to my student or back packing days.

Another option is to get a group together and hire an apartment. It is often cheaper but I would recommend making some suitable contacts first through a crew house.

Other options for looking for work are to go to Florida and Fort Lauderdale. There is a yacht show that takes place here every November which is good for day work and more permanent jobs. A word of caution here though, the Americans are highly strict on their visas and in order to work on a yacht you will require a B1 B2 visa. If you do not have one and start work, you face deportation and a ban from entering the country. I tried hard to get a B1 B2 visa, but was unable to without having a yacht to verify I would be working with them. I did read blogs online of people who managed to get their visas without a yacht, but I believe the system has become more regulated and obtaining one now without a yacht verifying your actions is near impossible.

Another option is to go to the Antigua Charter Yacht show in December. There are direct flights from London and no visa is required to enter the country on a British passport provided you have a return ticket back to the UK (check online for latest travel requirements). The yachts start arriving for the show towards the end of November. Though there is day work much of it will go to the locals making it harder to come by than in the Mediterranean.

Another consideration is to go to St Maarten in November as many yachts are on standby for the Caribbean season. Work does come up, not as frequently as in the Mediterranean, but there are always opportunities, often due to someone losing their job for excessive drunken antics! In St Maarten many of the ports have become stricter on who they allow in, therefore accessing the docks can be more difficult than in Europe. People do succeed and do get work and there are local agents here who can help (check online). It is also advisable to check with the local embassy with regards visa requirements

Palma in Majorca is another area to consider. I hear it is harder to access the marinas here with stricter security, making dock walking more difficult. Barcelona in Spain also has a busy ship yard, but like Palma, the security is strict and accessing the yard to dock walk is very difficult without being a named person on a yacht's crew list, which are kept with the security guards at the gate.

Without doubt my personal recommendation would be to go to Antibes in the South of France. It is easy to enter the country, convenient for accessing the UK, not too expensive to get to, has lots of crew agents and ports which permit dock walking allowing you to cover the four main ways of securing a job.

I would recommend getting there by March and book your accommodation in January. This way you can get into a crew house, meet people, start networking and pick up any jobs that may start coming in.

What Yacht to go for?

It is a very personal preference whether to opt for a charter yacht, a private one or one that does both. As someone new to the industry you may be less likely to have strong preferences and opt for the first offer of employment.

For me the most important element was the crew and if you are new to the industry this should be a major consideration.

Generally speaking the work on a charter yacht can be more demanding, although this is dependent on how popular it is bookings wise and what the clients are like. If it is a private yacht and the owners use it all through the season, you are going to find you are very busy indeed. A good indicator of the owners reputation is the longevity of the crew and this can provide a good overall indicator for any yacht.

Income potential on a private yacht will likely bring you more on your monthly salary though you are unlikely to be tipped (some owners do.) However on a charter your monthly salary may be less but you could easily double or triple your salary with tips during peak season.

There are differing views by crew members on the best size of yacht, certainly for a motor yacht the general impression I have is the optimum size is between 45 to 55 meters. This is a good size yacht, with between 8 to 18 crew and not too big to be impersonal. You get to know all the crew well and are often a close knit team. As a very general rule the charters tend to produce the best tip revenues for crew, though this is very much yacht and quality of crew dependent.

Yachts over 100 meters can easily have 30 to 70 plus crew and are often less personal. You may not get to know all the crew and may only socialise with a small group on-board. There may be a shift system in place for lunch with so many people to seat. You may only work in certain areas of the yacht, i.e. on one deck level.

At the opposite end (below 45 meters) the crew are often very close and smaller in number from a few to maybe 12. Crews work very closely together, often sharing roles. It can be better to start on a smaller yacht as you gain a broader range of skills to set you in a good stead for the future.

It can be a difficult choice as on seeing these beautiful yachts, human nature seems to attract to the largest or most attractive. However often the biggest and best may not suit, or you may not gel with that specific crew. Try to keep an open mind, treat each one as a potential opportunity and avoid becoming blinkered by appearances. I have had friends desperate to get on a yacht they have always admired, only to get on-board and leave within a couple of months as they are not happy. This is where day working and trial periods are beneficial as they give you a great opportunity to establish crews you could work with.

My advice would be, if possible, to familiarise yourself with the crew on-board first, look for crew longevity and ensure the reputation of the owners. If it is a charter yacht find out how many charters are booked, how the tips are split and be sure you are happy to work hard.

Some other important pointers to consider and work towards are listed below.

Appearance:

This is significantly important when looking for work. First impressions are important in an industry that so prides itself on image and appearance. Ensure you are clean shaven every morning you are looking for work and have clean and ironed clothes (without lots of logos.) I wore white polo shirts and navy blue shorts and smart non garish flip flops and tidy haircut. For girls it is advisable not to wear over the top make up or overly short skirts (whilst the latter may work on some captains it is better to look professional). Again a smart skirt, suitable length, or smart trousers and a white polo looks professional.

Carry your organised folder containing your CV, certificates, qualifications etc. and have spare CV's in case needed. Ensure the CV is stapled with two references at the back and the business card on the front; keep it neat and it will look very professional.

Commitment:

Use every available opportunity to find work and meet with all the agents you registered with. Commit to dock-walking every day, socialise and network with new people and following any potential leads. Work hard and get on well with others during any work onboard.

A Positive Attitude:

Trust me it can be difficult. When you are handing out lots of CV's and nothing seems to be happening. Keep putting in the hard work as it does pay off. It is often those that give up and not believing in their efforts that end up throwing in the towel. I vividly remember numerous down days when I felt I was banging my head against a wall. Then suddenly all can change. I had nothing for nearly two weeks, then in the space of 24 hours I had three fantastic opportunities to follow up. I had a day when two yachts asked me to do day work and another two offered permanent work. You really have to believe and stay as positive as possible.

Summary

Keep committed, keep smart, keep positive and keep focused on your end objective. In life I feel we make our opportunities and this is so true in yachting. The more you are there, handing out CV's, meeting agents, going to different ports, being seen, it is more likely that something will happen and an opportunity arise. Those who whinge about lack of jobs are often not making the opportunities and therefore not having breaks. There really is nothing greater than knowing your hard work has paid off. So throw off your bow lines, set your sails and head for your new adventure. Make the most of every chance, seek opportunity and accomplish a dream! Someone once said "To attract good luck to oneself it is necessary to take advantage of opportunities." How true that is.

I have enclosed some personal blogs detailing some of my experiences. I hope it gives you an insight and broadens your knowledge a little further. I have also enclosed an appendix with useful links as well as a copy of a blank CV.

My Final Thoughts:

Yachting has provided me with a great time. Sitting on the back of a super yacht watching the sun go down is a unique experience that only the super wealthy and crew may experience. However there have been times when I have hated the lack of personal space, missing family and friends and being told what to do.

Yachting has enabled me to save more than I could have in 15 years in my previous job and has set me up with a house deposit and more. It has provided me with some incredible memories, wonderful friends and taken me to some beautiful places. It has also taken me out of my comfort zone, proved you can achieve almost any goal you set yourself and has helped develop me as a person.

I personally chose not to make a career in yachting, realising that important things for me could not be provided on a yacht; namely friends and family. Whilst many people are able to juggle the two, for me I am too much of a home bird, loving the UK and home life and for that reason this would never be a long term option. However I have no regrets doing this, from my time spent out there and from the friends I have met. It is said that you regret the things you do not do far more than the things   you   do.

Good luck with whatever you decide, enjoy, be happy and I wish you smooth seas, lovely guests, great crews and happy and healthy times throughout.

Please feel free to contact me. While I cannot be putting your name forward for jobs, I will happily help with any unanswered questions or take on board anything you feel may be a useful addition to this guide.

Thank you for your time and interest and I wish you all the very best for your future ahead, wherever that may take you.

Ben Proctor

Ben_proctor@hotmail.com

www.workonasuperyacht.co.uk

https://www.facebook.com/workonasuperyacht

http://twitter.com/super_yachting

"It's not the blowing of the wind that determines your destination in life; it's the set of your sails."

Miles Hilton-Barber (A blind adventurer).

Please find the following selection of articles I have written about my time working on board, I hope you find these personal accounts a useful insight into the super yacht industry. Some of this work can be found at www.workonasuperyacht.co.uk

Deciding to Work on a Super Yacht?

Prior to leaving England on that cold wet day in September and embarking on my new adventure I spent a year considering the idea of working on a super yacht. I even spent a week in the South of France, chatting to yacht crews and others looking for work, all to help me decide if this was something I wanted to do. I vividly remember sitting on a beach in Antibes just off the harbour, writing out what seemed like an endless list of pros and cons…

The main problem with making the decision was that I seemed to have two voices in my head. One I called "Mr Sensible" and the other "Mr Adventurous" - both seemed equally logical and plausible depending on my mood, and were often influenced by the people I was surrounded by.

Mr Sensible would regularly tell me "you are in a well-paid secure job, have a nice apartment and all your friends around you. Why risk it all to work in an industry you have not experienced, to live in a small cabin, sharing with others, away from loved ones and may never even get a job on a yacht." All plausible reasons which moved the reality of my super yacht adventure further away.

The other side was Mr Adventurous, whose approach was much more exciting, maybe more risky but equally appealing. He would regularly say, "why stay in a job you don't like, while you have no commitments… explore the world, travel, have new experiences, save more money than you possibly could in your current job, meet new people, L I V E!!!"

Both would present highly convincing cases and my mind, for that year, felt like a high court case with the defendant and prosecution fighting to win. My mind was the jury.

Those I talked with also influenced my decision. My parents naturally opted for the safe and secure option, to stay in my current job, which was a sensible idea and a highly credible option. My friends encouraged me to "go, go, go" "what have you to lose". They would see more of the fun side of the adventure (travel, hot climates) and they all added support to Mr Adventurous.

I spent a week in France to help my decision and on arriving back in the UK headed straight to my work place. I met with my boss and told him my thoughts. On discussing my options he rightly said "what have you to lose." With no dependents, mortgage or ties he encouraged me to make the most of the opportunity He also reassured me my job would be there for me should things not work out. With that in mind I spoke to my family, who agreed with his sentiments and were equally encouraging. I realised where my heart lay and that I had a deep routed desire to give the super yacht world my best shot, stepping out of my comfort zone (something that I had not done for a long time) and challenge myself on this exciting yet unknown new path.

The decision was made, the jury in my mind quietened and a calmness came over me before the magnitude of my undertaking dawned on me. My mind buzzed with excitement, so much to sort and plan before leaving, courses to attend and tasks to complete, the first being my letter of resignation… this was really happening!

I handed in my notice the following morning giving four weeks notice. The month flew by and before I knew it I was sat on the tarmac at Bristol Airport in an Easyjet plane bound for Nice in the South of France.

I wish I could say I never regretted the decision but there were times when I did, on that plane, on first entering my crew dormitory, my first dock walk and many other occasions when Mr Sensible would question, "what are you doing?" I did have moments when I wondered if I had made the right decision; with people telling me how hard it was to get work and how I had left it too late to come to France. However, looking back on the whole experience it was certainly not the wrong decision and it has provided me with so many opportunities and memories that would never have happened had I not decided to take the big step that turned my career and life in a completely new direction.

Decisions at times can be very testing, and it is hard not to be influenced by the views of others, or the need to impress and please. Sometimes the easy decision is not necessarily the right one, leaving us stale and uninspired. It may seem more comfortable, certainly easier, though may not always bring happiness. Often the harder one may be worth making, taking you a little further out your comfort zone than you are comfortable with.

The power of one decision over another can have enormous consequences and change the path of your life in so many ways. I often wonder how my life would have been had I not chosen to take the chance of this great opportunity. It is hard to say, but I am sure it would not have included as many incredible sights, beautiful beaches, ports and towns, glorious sunsets and sun rises looking out over the sea, captivating wildlife, making friends and memories to last a life time.

I hope that in my twilight years I will remember some of the incredible moments from my time working on a super yacht and the happy memories and experiences gained. As for my office job... well I think I will have enough to relive without dwelling on this.

There is only one life and I sometimes feel we trade too easily our memories and moments at the expense of a pay cheque. Remembering time is finite and the need to appreciate every moment of each day may just help to create a future and past that you can look on with fondness and happiness.

Make the right decision; live, love, see, feel…enjoy a life you want to live and create your future as you want it.

"Your time is limited, so don't waste it living someone else's life. Don't be trapped by dogma – which is living with the results of other people's thinking. Don't let the noise of others' opinions drown out your own inner voice. And most important, have courage to follow your heart and intuition. They somehow already know what you truly want to become"

Steve Jobs

Dock Walking: My Personal Account of Dock Walking.

What is dock walking?

Dock walking is the process of walking along a dock, approaching a yacht, speaking with the crew with the aim of securing; day work, permanent work or to leave them with your CV.

For me this proved to be one of the most nerve wracking processes in finding work.

Monday morning 0630, I wake early in anticipation of the day ahead. I am living in a crew house with numerous other 'wannabe' super yacht crew all eagerly trying to secure a job, all competing for the same work on a limited number of yachts. I rise early to be the first in the shower for my first day walking the docks of Antibes. Presentation is important in this industry and my clothes are ironed and laid out the night before. I shower, shave and eat breakfast, my appetite is low as my nerves fill my stomach with a certain unease. I pack my bag with the essentials, sun cream and water, before leaving the crew house armed with a selection of recently printed CV's and references in a neat plastic folder. I want to be the first out of the crew house and onto the dock in the hope of catching any early crew out on deck.

It is a beautifully fresh morning and the salty smell of the sea lingers in the calm air that surrounds the small cobbled streets of Antibes. The sun is about to rise and the sky is clear with white aeroplane trails scarring the blue backdrop. There is a coolness in the air indicating an approach to Autumn. Leaving the cobbled streets I am greeted with a vast selection of yachts with the backdrop of a beautiful golden fort that overlooks the harbour of Antibes. The rising sun accentuates the golden colour of the fort. As I walk along the dockside a scavenging sea gull scurries into a hedge dragging some left over pizza from a torn bin bag. The water is calm and the town empty, it is 0730, the port is quiet.

I walk towards the International Dock which is the main dock, home to some of the largest super yachts in the world and pass the more modest yachts which by standards at home are still very impressive. My anxiety is growing as I approach the entrance, my heart races faster and my fears of rejection grow with every step. I pass the security barrier through an open gate looking like a boy about to embark on his first day at school, with rucksack, clean ironed clothes and carrying a folder of CV's. I certainly look like a novice. As I enter the International Dock I am greeted by a large yacht with the large letters 'D I L B A R' in gleaming silver. The reflection of the water glistens on the yacht's hull with the bow stretching way off into the distance. My heart beats rapidly and I almost try to convince myself that it is not a good day to dock walk: I will try tomorrow, it will be easier then... I know I must continue.

Sitting on the dock there is no-one around bar the security guard and he looks wholly uninterested in my intentions. I sit by a flower bed that overlooks the vast stretch of yachts all moored stern to dock. I struggle to comprehend the change in worlds I am experiencing in just two days. Two days ago I was working in an office watching the rain falling outside on a busy road... now I sit, unemployed, admiring these incredible yachts, with the blue sea and sky and the back drop of the old golden fort.

Slowly more dock walkers appear, some look highly experienced, walking with a certain confidence. Some I talk with politely and briefly though others are focused purely on the yachts and walk past without so much as an acknowledgement.

It is 0745 and I decide to walk to the opposite end and begin my walk from the far end, hoping to catch crews before they are disturbed by the other dock walkers. The larger yachts are at the beginning so I assume these will draw the most dock-walkers so I opt for the smaller yachts first (still over 60 meters in length). As I walk along the atmosphere starts coming alive with deck crew appearing from side doors and walking down the sides of the yacht. On the yacht next to me I notice a crew member (a moment I have long been anticipating) and my anxiety steps up another notch. I can feel my heart beating and blood pulsing around my body, a feeling I have not experienced since standing to do a best man's speech the month before. My mouth dries and I sweat as I approach the first yacht. The crew member appears to look at me, I think I have caught his attention. I smile, before he looks down and heads to the second deck to raise a flag. I am sure he noticed me but my polite English disposition stops me disturbing him and I convince myself they must be fully crewed and should therefore look elsewhere. As I walk away, I realise I have failed at the first hurdle in my search. With my disappointment building my heart rate eases a little and I continue along the dock, determined not to succumb to fear at the next one. I vow this will be the only yacht I do not approach ….a new beginning.

I approach the third yacht with grit and determination to find someone also putting out the flag and call up "are you looking for crew?" He looks down, smiles and informs me they are fully staffed. Although a rejection I feel an enormous sense of achievement. I have overcome my fear of asking for work and feel better equipped to start my search.

That morning I managed to talk to crew on five different yachts. Walking back to the crew house I felt more confident than I did starting out that morning and felt pleased to have given some CV's. I had completed my first mornings dock walking though many more lay ahead.

My dock walking skills improved with practice and it took about a week to feel more confident. I became slicker at asking if day work or crew were needed, and managed to leave more CV's and references even if they were not looking for crew at that time. I always tried to have a polite conversation before leaving, hoping to develop some rapport which I hoped would help me stand out from the crowd. I was delighted to find crews surprisingly helpful and welcoming. The reality is that most crews will have endured the process of dock walking themselves and know it is a necessary part of finding work, so empathise and help where they can.

My dock walking took me to many ports including Antibes, Cannes, Monaco, Nice and St Tropez, finding the best were Antibes and Monaco. I spent many hours and walked miles of docks handing out CV's and speaking to many crew. At times it did become disheartening when no leads came from my efforts. I always tried to remain positive and keep moving forward though it was difficult at times. I knew the clock was rapidly ticking, drawing a close to the end of another season when the yachts would start leaving the Mediterranean for the Caribbean.

However, the hard work, persistence and patience eventually paid off. I obtained day work on two yachts which helped build my CV making me far more employable.

Without realising it my quest for employment was coming to an end as I approached a yacht soon after it docked late one afternoon. My normal routine of enquiries followed with polite pleasantries while handing the crew member my CV. He asked about my qualifications and seemed disappointed I did not have a Yacht Masters certificate, informing me the Captain only employed deck crew with this qualification. I left disappointed as the yacht had an interesting itinerary and the crew seemed really friendly. The following morning on passing the same yacht the crew member called me over and offered me day work. This progressed from one days work to a week which lead to a trial period, and finally onto permanent work. All from that one fateful day speaking and handing my CV to that one member of staff.

It is such an incredible feeling achieving a job on a super yacht, completely off your own back after hours and hours of searching. Walking onto that yacht with all my possessions, from dock walker to full time crew member, was a day that filled me with great pride. Coming from an office job just two months earlier and stepping on board to start a new life working on one of the top charter super yachts in the world, was a moment in my life I will always remember and I felt a huge sense of achievement.

Looking back, the dock walking was the most nerve wracking part of the job-finding process. It did get notably better with time and practice once I had overcome the fear, and it really did get easier… I promise.

I wish you the very best of luck with this experience. Don't be timid, go for every yacht and seize every opportunity presented to you. Try to embrace any fear, for it is often the things that make us feel uncomfortable, fearful or nervous that can lead to some of the most exciting changes and opportunities in your life…

…you never know, that the one CV you hand to that one crew member could change the direction of your job search, put your dock walking days behind you and take your life to a whole new exciting adventure.

"To attract good luck to oneself, it is necessary to take advantage of opportunities"

George S. Glason.

My First 24 Hours Working on a Super Yacht.

The morning was fresh as I stepped out of the crew house with all my belongings crammed into my rucksack weighing heavy on my back. I made my way to Antibes station where I caught a train filled with commuters. I was heading for Genoa, a large mainly industrial port in Italy where a 54 meter yacht, which hires for over £300,000 per week, had offered me two weeks work.

Sitting on the train, I watched the beautiful coastline of the Cote D'Azur pass by as it hugged the coast and entered Italy, passing beautiful homes and small coves overlooking the electric blue Mediterranean Sea basking in bright sunlight. Looking at the view I felt more relaxed, knowing I have paid work for two weeks which will help me gain some much needed experience to build my CV to help secure that so far elusive permanent job.

Leaving the train at Genoa, I catch a taxi to the port. The taxi pulls up at the dock and before me lies a stretch of super yachts glistening in the afternoon sun.

I find the yacht and press the intercom system rigged at the end of the passerale. The buzzer rings and a polite girl answers. I savour what I know will be the last few moments of time on my own before I join the 16 full time crew I am to live and work with.

I am given a friendly welcome, asked to remove my shoes and step on-board...my first stride into the world of the super wealthy. I am led on board where the golden teak has a pleasant warmth underfoot and the glistening paintwork and railings sparkle like something from a fairy tale. There is an air of cleanliness on board, like a house after its annual spring clean. I am led to the back of the yacht, along the side, through a door, down some narrow steps and into the more humble living area of the crew mess. The crew are watching

TV and I am introduced to them all. I take in their names, believing I have stored these in my mind, only to realise that on shaking hands and thinking what to ask them next, I have not remembered one single name.

I am taken to my room via a narrow corridor lit with bright lights with numerous doors leading off and into a small room with three bunk beds. On top of my bed is a selection of uniform, two towels and bed sheets. I am shown my cupboard, consisting of a small hanging space and two shelves. The top bunk is to be mine which 20 years ago I would have argued over with my brother. Now I look on the practical side realising how hard it will be to go to toilet at night without stepping on the person below. The room has a small ensuite with shower, toilet and basin. I try the shower expecting a trickle of water, but am greeted with a powerful spray that splashes me and the surrounding floor. There are two small portholes, one in the ensuite and one in the bedroom, which provide a small amount of natural light and look out onto the neighbouring yacht and bluey green murky industrial water below.

I unpack and go to the crew mess to meet the crew who all seem friendly and encourage me to help myself to dinner. The meal is delicious and sheer luxury after three weeks living on pasta and sauce. I am shown around the crew quarters and take in the toiletries cupboard (a haven of the latest Lynx fragrance shower gels, top of the range Mach 3 Gillette razors and a host of other essentials to cater for any high maintenance grooming requirements!) I am told to help myself to whatever I choose; sheer luxury, and I spend a moment pondering which shower gel fragrance to opt for this time…

I am also told I can help myself to anything from the crew fridge and snack cupboard which resembles a mini candy and chocolate store crammed full. My eyes widen and stomach leaps with excitement as I glance at the extensive selection of treats.

I am also shown the crew entertainment system on the television and full Sky television which includes English channels as well as a stored library of almost every film I ever knew existed, all available at the press of a button. I am strangely pleased to see English television, I feel closer to home again.

Having sat in the crew mess for a few hours exchanging pleasantries whilst trying to watch the film, I decide to head to bed as the mornings early start and new experiences weigh heavy on my eyes.

I clamber onto the top bunk knocking my head in the process, a habit that will happen several times that week before I adjust to the restricted head room. I get into the clean sheets I made up some four hours previously and note that I am unable to sit up due to the lack of head room. I lie there, flick on the reading light, set my alarm and get ready to spend my first night on board.

The first night is an experience in itself. Lying there trying to sleep I mull over the change in my life in a relatively short space of time. There is a part of me excited at the future, but another part of me feeling wholly unsettled and unsure if this is the right thing to be doing in my late twenties. The thought of sharing my living space, room and essentially my life with these people makes me feel unsure and unsettled and I am wholly aware of how close the living quarters are and the little time and space there will be for myself. As someone who loves the company of others but relishes his own space, I am concerned this will be hard to settle in to.

I shut my eyes and notice the relatively subtle hum of the yachts air conditioning system and the crew mess TV in the background, accentuating every explosion Bruce Willis sets off during the Die Hard film. I gradually drift off to these noises.

I would like to say I awake to the sound of my alarm, but my sleep is disturbed by shutting doors in the crew area as others retire to their cabin. I am also woken each time I turn over, the bed being just wider than me, so turning becomes more of an art than ever before and I learn to sleep in an almost pencil-like formation, my days of "star fishing" in bed are now behind me.

The morning arrives, I wake before my alarm, draw my porthole curtain and lie in bed watching a couple of mullet fish cruising between our yacht and the next one. My relaxing is a mistake as I hear my roommate get up and lock the bathroom door. My planned shower, toilet and shave have been thrown as I realise that waiting for him will make me late, so I opt to dress and eat breakfast (note to self … establish showering times and get in the shower first tomorrow!)

A delicious breakfast with a selection of cereals, yoghurts and fresh fruit awaits. I then collect my radio and meet the Captain and deck crew on the bridge for a morning briefing of the day ahead.

I am given a tour of the whole yacht, something I have dreamt of since a small boy seeing these yachts in the South of France during a family holiday. The interior in the guest areas is a massive step up from the humble and compact crew areas. It is filled with high-class bespoke furniture, elaborate mirrors, glistening marble flooring, baths and beautiful wooden staircases. I feel I am on a photo shoot for an interior design magazine or elaborate film set; the style, taste and quality are like nothing I have witnessed before. I am shown into the main guest cabin complete with massive bed, walk-in dressing room, and an enormous ensuite with two large showers and a beautiful bath surrounded in white marble. Off the master bedroom is the sitting area where there is a discreet wall mounted button which when pressed creates a deep electrical buzzing noise before light begins to appear between the yacht's walls. As the side wall of the yacht lowers the buzzing stops and the wall is completely lowered to create a private balcony where the owner and guests can sit outside in complete privacy.

After seeing how the other half live I return to normality and my life as a deck hand. Today's job, I have been informed, is to wash the yacht…

Being a normal male, cleaning to an A1 standard did not come naturally, but as I was to learn quickly, this had to change. Prior to this I envisaged a "wash down" to be easy, akin to washing a car with a quick sponge and rinse. Not so. I was shown the process by the lead deck hand and taught that the yacht has to first be rinsed with fresh water to remove the salt or dirt to avoid scratching the paintwork. Next it is washed with a brush and mitten everywhere including doorways, deckhands (the ceilings on the outside decks) and even the gutters. The soapy water then has to be rinsed off before the water has time to dry otherwise it will leave unacceptable marks (no mean feat in temperatures of 28 degrees+). Finally, despite being in glorious sunshine, the whole yacht has to be dried with a shammy in stages to prevent water marks being left on the stainless steel or paintwork when it evaporates. I am told this process will take two to three days to complete and am dutifully given a mitten and told to start on the sun deck. I clarify where this "sun deck" is and negotiate my way up to the top deck.

I soon note the seemingly simple process of washing down a yacht may not be quite as simple as I hoped. I find I am continually making mistakes. I started drying the stainless steel before the deckhand, used a mitten to wash the side instead of a brush, left items on the deck that could mark the teak and wrang the shammy too hard before storing it. All these basic mistakes proved to me that even with A Levels and a degree, there is only really one way to learn, and that is by practice and experience. The reality of what this work entailed was rapidly sinking in and my illusions of driving tenders and jet skis for the rich and famous were rapidly fading. The crew were lovely but seemed to have missed the part of their training called 'positive feedback' and I was bombarded with criticism. I found this time hard, having come from a profession where I was advising people and being asked for my advice. I was continually making simple mistakes just washing an ornate object. It was a steep learning curve and I was just not used to being told what to do anymore. This had to change as I had much to learn.

The washing down routine was interrupted by very welcome breaks mid-morning, lunch time and mid-afternoon. Lunch was an incredible selection of dishes and salads laid out by the chefs which proved a real highlight from the days work. Also raiding the sweet and chocolate cupboard was another delight, without doubt replacing more calories than were burnt in the days activities.

The whole day was spent washing the yacht. It proved a good work out and having come from an office-based job I was loving the physical exertion. However the mundane nature of the job and the regular mistakes I was making was taking its toll and I finished the day with some serious question marks as to whether I had made the right career move.

After clearing away all the cleaning equipment, I returned to the crew area to tuck into another delicious meal. Afterwards I opted for a run around Genoa as I felt it important to spend at least a small part of the day off the yacht and relished the personal space whilst exploring the city. I returned from my run, showered and relaxed in the crew mess whilst watching a television program. The effects of the fresh air and physical work made my eyes feel heavy and my body pleasantly achy and I decided to head to bed early for what I knew was going to be a sound nights sleep.

Looking back, those first 24 hours were a total reality shock. All my questions on what working on a yacht would be like were answered and I must say there were many positives. Although my bed was small it was comfortable and the physical work certainly meant I slept well. The ensuite, although shared and small, worked really well after we developed a routine between us. The food was incredible. Furthermore, the endless supply of fragrant toiletries and products was a great luxury and I never tired of choosing them. As a crew member I was certainly very well looked after, living in this relatively confined space with 16 other people.

Those 24 hours were also a complete eye opener to the nature of the work and a far cry from the photos that I had seen on a friend's Facebook entries some four months earlier. The work was at times mundane, repetitive and had to be done in a specific way and to a very high standard. I had to learn to accept being told what to do and to take on board regular feedback from the mistakes made.

However, as with any new job, those initial weeks where you feel rather a spare part and a hindrance and question why you left your comfortable existence, slowly fade as you take on more responsibility and work becomes second nature.

There were times in those initial two weeks where I seriously considered returning home, back to the comfortable surroundings and a world where I was in control and knew my trade. However pride, stubbornness and a fear of failure kept me there and made me work hard. I knew there would be better times and I was right to believe this.

Never could I have known where these two weeks experience would lead me. Without a doubt this was my springboard to launch me into the world of super yachts. It provided me with all the essential skills I needed for my CV and I was so fortunate to be part of a yacht that trained me so well with such a competent crew.

Little did I know, as I stepped off this yacht at the end of my time, that in just four weeks I would be stepping onto another yacht to become my home for over two years and take me to some of the most incredible places on earth.

My Top 3 Highs of Working on a Super Yacht

1) Watching dolphins bow riding the yacht's wake.

Being out in the vastness of the sea and hearing the call on our radios that dolphins were around always brought a sense of urgency and excitement to the crew, even the more salty sea dogs. Watching these incredible creatures bow riding the waves with such effortless ease and grace, darting left and right, diving deeper and then breaching the white wash, was always an incredible sight. Their almost human-like facial expressions and deep dark eyes would captivate us whilst they graced us with their presence. It is a picture that I often think of and will stay with me as one of those very special life moments.

2) Time on deck alone when underway.

I worked with some incredible crew and am not a social recluse, however living with people in relatively close living quarters, to have time on your own can be magic. Some of my highlights were leaving the South of France en route to Corsica when on anchor duty. The foredeck was empty and on the horizon sat the most perfect golden sun as it slowly descended. I had wind in my face and the sound of the yacht's bow slicing through the waves. As I sat there I savoured every moment as the sun drew a close to another day.

There were also times when I would sit on the top deck (it had three) and watch the sun set over the vast expanse of white wash created by the yacht. From this elevation it felt as though I had a bird's eye view over its wake and the distant horizon and sunset.

Other memorable times were standing just outside the bridge on the many night passages of an Atlantic Ocean crossing, hearing the waves running along the side and looking up to the most brilliant stars I have ever seen. This was an incredible spectacle, making me appreciate not only the vastness of the world but the incredible simplistic beauty that lies around us, something we so often take for granted.

These were all magical moments experienced from incredible surroundings of the yacht, taking me to some of the most wonderful, and at times most peaceful places in the world.

   3) Swimming with turtles.

This was a childhood dream for me and something I had always wanted to do having seen one in an aquarium. One of my crew located the turtles who seemed to be attracted to some underwater grass. I first heard a chewing noise before seeing the dark figure on the sea bed. Slowly approaching the turtle I hovered above. He seemed wary of me though the distance between us seemed to provide him some comfort. Chewing the sea grass he would regularly twist his long aged neck to look at me as though checking out my intentions. I pushed my luck and dived down for a closer look and as the water flowed into my snorkel it made a bubbling noise causing the turtle to look up, and with a big swish of its large front legs it shot off. I followed, kicking my legs and flippers as hard as I could, but it glided away with such grace, effortlessly moving through the water. I kicked as hard as I could until I could hold my breath no more…as I came to the surface I saw the dark figure glide into the even darker abyss. It was an incredible sight to witness a turtle in its natural environment, this prehistoric looking creature that appears so well suited to living at sea but cumbersome when waddling up the beach.

I feel very fortunate to have witnessed so much wildlife during my time away, such an incredibly positive element to the whole experience and one I truly relished.

Whilst planning to only choose my top three experiences I felt I could not fail to mention some of the memories I made from time spent with my crew. Working closely with people in such an intimate way is a challenge for anyone and I was always so lucky with those I was fortunate to work with. There is certainly a mundane element to some of this work, cleaning a yacht can wear thin, but so often we would have some of the best laughs during these more mundane times. There was certainly a great camaraderie and banter. We had some fantastic meals out as a crew, went to several lovely beach clubs, spent some amazing days exploring new and exciting places and experienced many highs and lows together. It can at times be challenging and there will be disagreements, but it is people that make daily life more interesting and fulfilling, and working together in such close proximity has far more positives than negatives. I have some very happy memories and know they would not shine so brightly were it not for the fantastic crew I shared so many of these experiences with.

My Top Three Lows of Working on a Super Yacht.

1) Christmas.

I always found this a difficult time to be away from home and believe most crew would agree. One especially stands out... Christmas morning 2011 on a crossing from St Maarten to St Barts, a call came over the radio for a deck crew member to go to the bridge deck. Hoping it may be a Christmas treat I rush up only to be greeted by a large area of vomit on the yachts pristine teak decking. I clean the deck, scrubbing and rinsing down, while the yacht gently lurches from side to side, spreading what was already a sizeable area into an even larger one. Rinsing it down I feel a small sense of satisfaction as I near the end of this less than appealing task, only to notice in the scuppers (the drains around the side of the decks) that some of the larger chunks are too big to enter the drains. With plastic gloves, kneeling and clearing chunks of vomit, I decide this is not one of the high points in my life.

2) Missing my brother's first child being born.

I was delighted to hear that the baby had been born safely but it was difficult not being there for my first niece coming back to our family home with everyone there. Having met her three months later it was clear she would have no idea who was around at the time of her birth. However it is one of those special events to share with your brother and be a part of. My sister-in-law reassured me I was seeing her at a much more interesting stage three months later which was of some comfort. It was always one of the things I found hard to accept, putting the yacht, an innate object, ahead of family and friends, controlling your life. I also missed close friends' weddings when we had guests on board and were not permitted leave. It is one of the sacrifices that comes with the job and though I learnt to accept found it very difficult. For many crew it is the one thing that pushes them away from this industry.

3) Working hard on a charter and not receiving a guest tip.

This sounds very spoilt and ungrateful, and I nearly omitted it here as so many people do incredible jobs with no tips and deserve them more than we as crew ever did. However I wanted this to be honest so included it being a genuinely low point for us all, despite working the hardest and longest hours of any prior trip. For one reason or another we did not receive a tip. It sounds awful but money does become a big part of life working on a yacht, probably too big, with some putting money above everything else. But the rewards compensate for the hard work, long hours and sacrifices made and becomes that carrot at the end of a stick making up for the less appealing side of the job. These three weeks were hard work and to make matters worse it was over Christmas and New Year, a time when we all wanted to be at home with loved ones. In reality we had been anticipating something in the region of £4000-£5000 but it never materialised. This had a really bad effect on crew morale and relationships, and people started blaming others for not getting the expected reward. I feel guilty to say but this was one of the low points, especially when there are far more serious problems in the world and others doing such worthy works without financial incentives…maybe it just shows what a focus money had become to us all.

Christmas on a Super Yacht.

I always found it difficult being away from home for Christmas. You are likely to be in a hot climate (the Caribbean or Florida) and having grown up in England, experiencing Christmas in the heat for me is not right, let alone seeing an inflatable snowman bobbing away on a Caribbean beach with temperatures of 35 degrees. It just doesn't seem to have the same kind of magic.

Then comes the fact that you are away from home and for me and the crews I worked with, no other time made you feel so far away and miss your loved ones so much. There is something about Christmas, the magic of leaving work on Christmas Eve, driving back to your family, catching up with loved ones, sharing presents and laughter and relaxing around those dear to you (and yes, watching the same episodes of Only Fools and Horses and the Queens speech.)

Christmas and New Year are very popular times for guests and owners to use their yachts, so it is often a very busy time on board – no relaxing in a beach club drinking rum punches with the crystal clear Caribbean water lapping at your feet.

The reality of Christmas on a super yacht is not all bad though. For most crew and certainly those I worked with Christmas was celebrated a week or two earlier. From my personal experience this would consist of an incredible roast dinner, not only roast turkey, but beef and ham, with every trimming you could imagine. This would be eaten outside on the second deck around the main guest table, looking out onto the glorious bright blue sea over the distant hills of St Maarten in the Caribbean. The deck would be filled with chatter, laughter and the sounds of Slade and Band Aid playing through the air. Alcohol would flow, wines and beers all provided by the yacht would lap on top of your ever expanding waist line as you indulged in this glorious feast. An incredible selection of puddings would follow with Christmas pudding and chocolate log among the favourites.

Following this one of the crew would dress as Santa and give out the presents from the yacht. Often thoughtful gifts such as shorts, swimwear, t-shirts, flip flops and even once a voucher from a local gentleman's club nearby. A kind gesture which was always gratefully received. Many also provide an additional months salary (those I worked on did) and this was an extra generous gift.

I also heard stories of crew being given jewellery, watches (Omega and Rolex for those lucky ones) and iPads. These more lavish gifts were often given to crew on private yachts where they became better acquainted with their owners, spending longer times together on board.

After this over indulgence and festive cheer we would go to a local bar for a few rum punches and Caribbean cocktails - drinking and dancing until the early hours. We all knew that this was likely to be our last drinking session for a while as our preparation for the guests arrival would soon start.

The organising for the guests arrival would generally start a couple of weeks beforehand. We always felt we had so much time to get everything done, but it was amazing how quickly the days flew by and we often ended up working longer hours to ensure everything was completed. Duties included washing and drying the entire yacht, cleaning all stainless steel and masts, polishing all the windows and name plates, as well as loading crew and guest supplies for the coming weeks. It was a busy time but everyone pulled together. On falling into bed I would browse Facebook and see the exciting flurries of posts and photos of people back home with loved ones, on country walks, in the pub, wrapped up warm, and together.

I would always try to call home before guests arrived on Christmas Eve because once there your time was their time, so it did not give you the luxury of personal space. This contact home was one of the things I loved to do, but at the same time it also pulled on the heart strings that bit more. It was always lovely to hear their voices and see them on skype and certainly while speaking you felt that bit closer... but this soon ended upon hanging up. My mother would often try to hide her emotions on the other end but it was always clear and moving to hear the break in her voice as we wished each other a happy Christmas and sent our love before we ended the call.

The guests would often arrive in a selection of mini bus vans with the principle guests in blacked out Mercedes. As soon as the cars drove along the dock we switched into work mode. Christmas Eve was here but not in the true sense of home. We would welcome guests with a cheerful smile and eagerness to help.

Christmas day would arrive to an early start, a quick shower and up on deck to start a list of duties before guests surfaced. Behind the scenes in crew areas there was always a slightly subdued atmosphere being Christmas day, an unspoken loneliness away from loved ones, while in front of guests we covered up our emotions with our eager to help cheerful faces. The day would come and go, and to be honest, for us deck crew, it felt much like any normal day of the year on charter, working 12-16 hours. I always enjoyed getting to bed knowing that another Christmas had passed.

Each Christmas I vowed would be my last, but with time you forgot how it felt being away from home and before you knew it another one was fast approaching. These times did not get any easier, regretfully they seemed to get only harder.

It is a strange time being away but I felt very fortunate to be living in such good conditions and being looked after so well. Many peoples' jobs force them away for Christmas, working in far worse conditions with less access to speak to loved ones - so in that respect I felt very fortunate. We were always well looked after and the yacht's management did their best to provide us with some form of Christmas celebration. But for me Christmas was and always would be the hardest time and the furthest I ever felt away from home, family and friends.

However, looking back I appreciate my time away at this period as it has made me appreciate those I love and how very precious time is when with them. So if you do ever spend Christmas away, just know that your next one at home will be all the richer.

Working as a Couple on a Super Yacht?

This article was written in response to a question from someone who read my book. I hope it may be useful to some of you reading this now.

Working on a yacht as couple can not only be a test but an incredible time to strengthen a relationship. If you can work together in such close proximity then it is a good indication of something special. It can also provide you both with a great set of life skills and an incredible financial future. I have met several couples who make it work really well.

Options for finding work as a couple on a yacht:
Some couples look for jobs expressing clearly they are looking for work together. It normally comes down to a Captain's preference whether he/she accepts couples. While this may limit your options it also stands you in good stead to achieve what you both want. Another option is to find work as a single person, work hard to establish a good reputation, build experience and then approach the Captain when someone leaves to see if they can get their partner on board. As new crew the latter option will more likely increase both your chances and potentially lead to a job together in the future on either of your yachts (you would be unlucky for both yachts to not take couples).

The larger yachts generally have a bigger staff turnover so these may be good to focus on. They also allow more space from one another if needed. However I do have friends who run a small yacht as a couple, this situation being much more intimate.

I would see what jobs are offered to you as an individual, look to get your foot in the door, see whether couples are an option and if any crew are leaving. Often a permanent position will not be offered immediately only day work or a trial period. This is therefore a great opportunity to get a feel for the yacht and see whether your partner joining may be an option. If you/your partner get a job first and can establish a good reputation the Captain will not want to lose you and an opening may therefore evolve.

Another option is to be completely honest and look for jobs purely as a couple and not consider anything else. It will probably take longer but you may be happier. Perhaps set a time frame for this then if no luck look for work separately.

Once you both have a season or twos experience behind you getting work together should be much easier. You may need to look on it as a short term sacrifice for the longer term gain.

There really is no right or wrong way or hard and fast rule. Sometimes it is being in the right place at the right time.

Good luck with your careers together.

Super Yachts and the Economy

I was at a social event recently when the conversation came around to my work in the super yacht world. Much to my surprise I was abruptly given the person's view on these yachts and dutifully told how obscene was the waste of money and how wrong it was that these yachts were allowed to exist.

To be honest this was a view I shared when I started work, but I began to see the other side on experiencing this life and meeting people in the industry.

Yes, the wealth needed to run a super yacht is hard to comprehend and of course there are so many worthy causes that could be helped from what it costs to keep one running. However they provide work to so many.

These yachts have saved many ship yards from bankruptcy as commercial work dried up, with many facing certain closure. The industry has provided new seeds of hope and as it has grown has created a booming industry for ship yards and skilled labour alike.

It has allowed small businesses to grow and support massive networks of people and families, giving people the chance to create a business from scratch and build it into something the owner can be proud of. I met many people who had developed a small family business to cater for the large super yacht industry, with a growing number of employees.

These yachts provide generous incomes for the crew which can provide, even the most junior crew, with the opportunity to save for a more financially secure future. I managed to save enough money to secure a sizable deposit for a house, helping me achieve a foot on the property ladder, which before my time away was proving too difficult.

Also the yachts run numerous charity events. There would often be donations at the end of yacht shows, where crews and yachts would give generous donations to excellent local causes. Often crews would set up challenges on-board such as using a rowing machine for the entire duration of an Atlantic crossing, "rowing the Atlantic", raising lots for charity. On top of this charity work is the incredible charity project that some of the super wealthy run, a well known one being The Bill and Melinda Gates Foundation http://www.gatesfoundation.org/ and The Giving Pledge http://givingpledge.org/

Many yachts are now working to offset some of their carbon footprint by providing generous donations to support green projects to help counter CO_2 level rises and renewable energy sources around the world.

The number of lives that these yachts have changed in a positive way is vast and this list is by no means exhaustive, but I hope from looking at the other side you can appreciate the immensely positive aspect to these yachts and the benefits they can have on many peoples lives all around the world. It has been reported that up to $250,000 can be injected into the local economy by guests and crew on a single visit from a super yacht…and that surely has to be a good thing.

The Cost of Running a Super Yacht:

Figures within the super yacht industry are hard to comprehend. Below is a guide that will give you an introduction into the world you could soon be entering.

Fuel:

I always found it hard to come to terms with the cost of the fuel used by these huge vessels. As an approximate guide a yacht of 70 meters will consume about 500 litres of diesel an hour when the engines are running but <u>not</u> moving! The cost of a yacht moving will be approximately £2,000 an hour to achieve cruising of around 18 knots. With this in mind the average overnight cruise of 12 hours could cost around £24,000 (this will be significantly higher for the larger yachts).

Berthing:

Berthing is certainly no cheap feat. Some top ports charge €2,000-€3,000 per night. The six most expensive are 1) Capri, Italy 2) Porto Cervo, Italy 3) Portofino, Italy 4) Ibiza Magna, Ibiza 5) St Tropez, France 6) Port Hercule, Monaco. The mooring cost is normally based on the yacht's size and popular ports are booked months in advance in peak season. A yacht also needs to be moored when on standby. Ports such as Antibes charge up to €2,000 per night, or renting a permanent dock here (as some owners do) costs hundreds of thousands. If like Roman Abramovich you build one of the biggest super yachts in the world, it is then difficult to actually find a port that can accommodate this size. At one stage it was reported he was to pay to have a dock extended, however he eventually found a couple of ports that could accomodate it.

Crew:

Captains salaries alone can exceed €20, 000 per month, and some chief engineers may earn €10, 000 per month …very quickly vast funds mount up just to keep the yacht fully crewed. Wage bills of €100,000 per month are not uncommon on the larger yachts. As well as the crew on board there may also be shore based crew, managing agents, financial staff etc. to add to this figure. There is also the cost of providing food, toiletries and all living requirements for the crew. Feeding 50 people on a daily basis is no cheap undertaking.

Servicing:

The servicing costs of these yachts are huge. Lifting them out the water is not cheap and to service these technological advanced super structures and engines there is a hefty price tag. Servicing costs for the larger yachts easily run into millions of pounds annually.

Super Yacht Toys:

Add to all these costs the need for the latest toys and gadgets on board.

The best looking, most advanced tenders are frequently custom built and often exceed the £1 million bracket. Coupled with the essential need for the latest jet skis, helicopters, submarines, diving equipment and numerous other toys to make your yacht complete.

Safety and Security:

Attacks from pirates is a growing threat and owners are all to weary of ensuring their pride possession is not held ransom in foreign waters. Equipment such as lasers that can cause temporary loss of vision cost some €70,000 from SeaLase and demand for their product is reportedly growing. Another product is the $450,000 "SeaOwl" tracking system, which combines radar and infrared or thermal cameras to detect incoming threats as far as five kilometers away. On top of these are the panic rooms, anti-paparazzi shields and armed security staff.

To cover the running and maintenance costs of a super yacht it is recommended that some 10-12% of the purchase cost is allowed. Therefore a £50 million yacht is likely to cost around

£5 million a year to run and maintain. The largest yachts have been reported to be costing their owners over €50 million a year.

It has been estimated that the average yacht is used for some three to five weeks a year, so justifying such a purchase to your accountant as a sound financial investment may prove difficult!

With costs like this it is easy to see why some of these yachts are hired for over £1 million a week by guests. Such a cost in the grand scheme of owning a yacht could almost be deemed value for money. Chartering the yacht also provides some income to those owners not using theirs on a regular basis.

Owning a super yacht must be one of the ultimate distinguishing marks of achievement that money can buy, but once purchased it can be seen that the costs will continue into the millions to run and maintain one.

Understanding the Super Wealthy

I always found it difficult to comprehend the wealth of the owners and those chartering these yachts. Looking online I found some useful everyday comparisons which show the incredible leap from millionaire to billionaire, way higher than I ever imaged.

Hopefully you will find the below examples useful in helping understand the super wealthy and appreciating the level of wealth of some you may meet.

A million:

- One million is a thousand thousands.
- One million is a 1 with six zeros after it, denoted by 1,000,000.
- One million seconds is about 11 and a half days.
- One million pennies stacked on top of each other would make a tower nearly a mile high.
- If you earn $45,000 a year, it would take 22 years to amass a fortune of one million dollars.
- One million ants would weigh a little over six pounds.
- One million dollars divided evenly among the U.S. population would mean everyone in the United States would receive about one third of one cent.

A billion:

- One billion is a thousand millions.
- One billion is a 1 with nine zeros after it, denoted by 1,000,000,000.
- One billion seconds is about 31 and a half years.

- One billion pennies stacked on top of each other would make a tower almost 870 miles high.

- If you earn $45,000 a year, it would take 22,000 years to amass a fortune of one billion dollars.

- One billion ants would weight over 3 tons - a little less than the weight of an elephant.

- One billion dollars divided equally among the U.S. population would mean that everyone in the United States would receive about $3.33.

Quite a sharp difference, so when talking about millions to run a yacht, for a billionaire this is relative pocket money in comparison.

I hope you find the above articles of use, providing an even more personal account to help you on your journey. If you think of any other topics that would be useful to read about then please email me on Ben_proctor@hotmail.com

Article Written for Escape the City, published 30 July 2014.

FROM OFFICE JOB TO WORKING ON A BILLIONAIRE'S SUPER YACHT.

Why did I escape?

Prior to my escape I was in a successful job as a case manager, earning a good salary, but deep down I was not content. I found work in an office mundane, it lacked any excitement, change of routine or dynamism. I often found my mind and eyes wondering outside, looking at the grey rain falling onto the grid-locked road outside. I realised I was stuck in a rut and no longer living life to the full. Alongside this I had an uneasy feeling that I was not ready to settle down, maybe I was going through my first very early mid-life crisis!

Before making the leap I fought on a daily basis with what to do, with Mr Sensible saying "stay in your secure 9-5 job" or Mr Adventurous saying "get out of your rut, explore, just do it". I knew in my heart which was right, but it is strange how much weight we put on a mundane safe existence in today's society, even if that course does not make you happy or feel alive. So in what some would describe as a moment of madness or, as it felt to me a moment of clarity I handed in my notice and embarked on a new world, career and a completely new lifestyle.... a world in which I was a complete novice.

My Escape into the Super Yacht World

I completed some professional qualifications and caught a plane to the South of France, heading to a port called Antibes; a beautiful fortified town, home to some of the largest super yachts in the industry. With no job prospect, no experience of working on a super yacht and just a ruck-sack of belongings I booked into a crew house and my dormitory room ...... quite a change from my secure job and the harbourside apartment I left some 24 hours earlier. Doubts were strongly ringing as the reality of my move abroad set in.

Finding work proved a full time job for nearly two months, meeting with crew agents, networking at social gatherings, and walking miles of docks handing out CV after CV. It was a hard step down from a profession where I was nearing the top of my career to essentially cold-calling to secure a job I had no experience in. At times it seemed relentless, with nothing developing from what I hoped would be many positive leads. Persistence and hard work eventually paid off and I slowly made inroads and started to get some interest.

I secured day work on a couple of super yachts, leading to two weeks work and eventually I achieved my goal, working on one of the top super yachts as a deck hand (available to hire at close to half a million euros per week, a price I still struggle to comprehend.)

What did my new life consist of?

My work varied but when guests were on-board I would tend to their requests sometimes teaching them water sports and ferrying them around on high speed tenders (small speed boats) to beautiful ports and beaches. The work also involved a great deal of cleaning and maintaining the yacht to an extremely high standard, a new skill I had to develop as cleaning was not a natural forte of mine! The view from my office was quite a contrast to the grid locked road of my previous job.....one day I would be working with the backdrop of Monaco, then looking onto the Amalfi coastline the following day, one day could be spent whizzing around on jet skis, the next day up a mast polishing stainless steel.

During my time I was fortunate to experience four Atlantic crossings, and saw most of the Caribbean and Mediterranean. I saw some incredible sights; from the most amazing sunsets, dolphins bow riding the yachts wave and whales breaching in the yachts wake, to the most brilliant bright stars I have ever seen in the middle of the Atlantic. At times the hours were long, especially when guests were on-board but the negatives were massively outweighed by the people I met, the sights I saw and the memories I treasure. It was an incredible time.

What my escape taught me?

In hindsight, the day I handed in my notice was one of the best decisions I have made so far in my life. Sometimes it seems easier to continue life unchanged, with the security around us in employment, home and friends. However stepping out of your comfort zone can open up a whole new world, endless exciting opportunities and create memories to last a life time.

Looking back and reflecting, there are so many potential opportunities thrown at us each day and changing one decision can have consequences that take us into a whole new direction and life. I wonder how many opportunities like this I have closed the door on through fear, doubt and a will to keep to my safe existence. I have learnt to say yes more and not be afraid of embracing new experiences. We only have one life and it is up to us to make it a journey to remember.

"Risks"

To laugh is to risk appearing the fool.
To weep is to risk appearing sentimental.
To reach out to another is to risk involvement.
To expose feelings is to risk exposing your true self.
To place your dreams, ideas before a crowd is to risk their loss.
To love is risk not being loved in return.
To live is to risk dying.
To hope is to risk despair.
To try is to risk failure.
But risks must be taken, because the greatest hazard in life is to risk nothing.
The person who risks nothing, does nothing, has nothing, and is nothing.
They may avoid suffering and sorrow, but they cannot learn, feel, change, grow, love, live.
Chained by their attitudes, they are a slave: they have forfeited their freedom.
Only a person who risks is truly free.

By William Arthur Ward

Yachting Terms

I would recommend getting a basic understanding of nautical terms by searching online or purchasing one of numerous nautical applications downloadable to a smart phone. It would also be beneficial if considering working as part of deck crew to look at some basic knots, paying special attention to a Bowline, Round Turn and a Half Hitch, Sheet Bend, Clove Hitch and a Figure of Eight knot.

Aft: Towards back of boat

Bit: Often stainless steel in nature, used to tie off the main line to the yacht, usually in figure of eight pattern.

Bow: Front of the yacht

Bridge deck: This is the deck level from where the boat is driven (i.e. the bridge). Often there is a deck at the back, known as the bridge deck aft.

Capstan: Electrical device used to pull tension into main lines which turns clockwise or anticlockwise.

Deck Checks: Process by which a crew member checks all decks whilst guests use them, to ensure high standards of cleanliness and presentation are maintained. This includes restocking towels, straightening/tidying cushions, clearing glasses/plates, topping up/cleaning Jacuzzi and cleaning marks off decks, stainless steel or paintwork. This is often not as tedious a job as it sounds if attractive guests are on-board!

Forepeak: Deck storage area at front of yacht.

Fore-deck: The deck area at the front of the yacht. This area has the winches and capstans for anchors and any lines at the front of the boat.

Forward: Closer to front of boat

Galley: The kitchen.

Head: Toilets

Heaving lines: These are small lines that are used during docking, approximately ten meters in length with a form of weight at one end. The non-weighted end is attached to the eye of the main line that will be used to moor the yacht to the dock. The other weighted end is thrown to the team on the dock who pull the line which pulls the larger main line to the dock.

Lazarette or garage: Storage space for water sports equipment e.g. tenders, windsurfers, kayaks, life jackets etc.

Main Deck: This is the deck that is normally entered from the passerale. It is the lowest outside deck (not including the swim platform)

Master Cabin: The best, often largest cabin on-board, where the owner will stay or principal guest.

Passerale: The walkway leading from the lower outer deck (main deck) to the dock. This is normally electric and at the back of the boat often on just one side, but may be port or starboard side.

Port: The left side of the boat as you look towards the front.

Principal Guest: Person paying to charter the yacht.

Scuppers: The drain that runs around the edge of the decks where the water runs.

Squeegee: The plastic blade with rubber like end, used with a pole to remove excess water from the decks, often used once they have been rinsed.

Starboard: The right side of the boat as look forward to the bow

"There is no RED PORT LEFT in the bottle." With this remember that the light to indicate the port is RED and the side port is on is the LEFT. You then know that the starboard side has to be RIGHT and the light colour (as there is only a red and green) has to be GREEN! It may just help you.

Stopper Lines: Small lines (less than one meter) which are used so the main line to the dock can be transferred from the capstan to the bit.

Sundeck: The top deck that gets the most sun. Motor yachts normally have a sundeck forward (towards front) and sundeck aft (towards back). Some of the larger boats may have larger decks where guests can sunbathe and drink from bars.

Swim Platform: The lowest deck, normally used purely for water sports, swimming and tender runs.

VIP cabin: The guest cabin that is usually the second best cabin after the master cabin.

Whips: Poles that extend off the side of the boat with lines that are attached to the tenders. These keep the tender parallel to the yacht yet are far enough away so as not to damage it. With the lines it is possible to pull the tender alongside.

Useful Links:

Please also visit my website which contains some of the links below:

www.workonasuperyacht.co.uk

FURTHER INFORMATION AND HELP

Super Yacht UK: A very good website offering useful information with a good career section.

http://www.superyachtuk.com/

http://www.superyachtjobs.com/

Other career information can be found at:

http://www.camperandnicholsons.com/superyacht-crew/yacht-crew-career.htm

Dockwalk Magazine: This is a great magazine for crew. It has really helpful topics and general crew and yachting information. I registered for the emails and magazines (available free online). Excellent information for getting an insight into the industry.

http://www.dockwalk.com/

Anther useful magazine aimed for crew is the following:

http://www.thecrewreport.com

UKSA offer this helpful document for more information:

http://uksa.org/wp-content/uploads/2013/11/UKSA-Guide-to-yachting.pdf

Other websites that may be of help:

http://www.workonaboat.com/

CREW ACCOMODATION:

Crew Grapevine in Antibes. Good, clean, nice showers, internet, wash facilities etc., (see the website). The owners are helpful and professional. They now own two crew houses, the Portside and the Seaside.

http://www.crewgrapevine.com/

Glamorgan: Also has a very good name in the industry.

http://www.theglamorgan.com/

FIANANCE:

Seafarers tax rules by the tax office (HMRC)

http://www.hmrc.gov.uk/cnr/seafarerstax.htm

I used SK Tax to deal with declaring my earnings for tax purposes at the recommendation of my Captain. I found them very helpful and knowledgeable.

http://www.sktax.co.uk/

MARITIME LABOUR CONVENTION 2006:

http://www.itfseafarers.org/ITI-IMO-ILO.cfm

http://www.ilo.org/global/standards/maritime-labour-convention/lang--en/index.htm

This is likely to have an impact on hours of work for crew, the rights of crew as well as well-being and living conditions. The effect and impact of this in the super-yacht industry will be interesting to see. Improvements in living conditions for crew are already implemented on newly built yachts.

CREW AGENTS:

You will determine which agents you prefer and find most efficient. The first two agent links listed were the ones I favoured. Everyone will have different views and preferences based on personality and experience and your relationship with that particular agent. It is advisable to register with each agency online before you leave. Most of the agencies use an online system on which you will need to register, showing you are looking for work. You should login at least two days when there. After meeting your agent it is advisable to keep contact weekly. The recruitment agencies are as follows:

YPI Crew: http://www.ypicrew.com/

Blue Water: http://www.bluewateryachting.com/

JF Recruiting: http://www.jf-recruiting.com/crew_reg/registration.asp

Crew Unlimited: http://www.crewunlimited.com/crw_register.asp

Camper Nicholson: http://www.camperandnicholsons.com/superyacht-crew/yacht-crew-registration.htm

Cosmo Crew: http://www.cosmo-crew.com/registration.html

Y Crew: https://www.ycrew.com/

Luxury Yacht Group: https://www.luxyachts.com/crew/crew_register.aspx

CREW TRAINING:

STCW 95 training in Antibes (book before you leave if planning to do this when there, as it will be busy during peak season.

http://www.bluewateryachting.com/crew-training/stcw-95-basic-training

UKSA: A well established and respected training centre which runs courses on the Isle of Wight.

http://www.uksa.org/career/mca/stcw-95/stcw-95-basic-training.asp

Also on the Isle of Wight:

http://www.redensigntraining.com/products/stcw95/stcw-95-basic-safety-training-week.aspx

All the courses follow a similar structure. I chose the most convenient location for me and went with Cornish Cruising, who ran a good course with a well organised and efficient format.

http://www.cornishcruising.com/stcw95

For your local provider you may find it at the following site.

http://www.alphatozulu.com/tuition/stcw_95.html

Other courses available:

Below is a selection of the training centres which offer a selection of maritime related courses, suitable for super yachts.

http://www.bluewateryachting.com/crew-training/courses

http://www.uksa.org/career/yachting/yachting-course-navigation.asp

It is best to select the course which appeals and will be the most relevant to the position you are applying for. There are numerous websites to search. Do not be afraid to contact an agent and ask which they recommend. Remember that an STCW is a legal requirement for working on a yacht over 24 meters and you will not be employed without this.

Royal Yachting Association (RYA) has a useful website on yachting relating topics and courses:

www.rya.org.uk

VISA REQUIREMENTS

Antigua Visa Requirements:

http://www.antigua-barbuda.com/travel_tourism/information/passport_visa.asp

THE SUPERYACHT MARKET:

To familiarize yourself with the yachts the following links may be useful:

Superyacht Times: Provides a comprehensive coverage of most the superyachts and is a great way to view them.

http://www.superyachttimes.com/

Top 100 Super yachts:

http://www.superyachts.com/largest-yachts/worlds-largest-yachts-live.htm

You can also visit the Charter Broker sites directly using the following.

http://www.camperandnicholsons.com/yacht-charter/index.htm

http://www.ypigroup.com/yacht-charter/index.htm

http://www.bluewateryachting.com/

Example CV:

Joe Bloggs

Address: *INSERT*

Date of birth: INSERT

Phone: INSERT

Email: *INSERT*

Nationality: *INSERT*

Marital Status: Single

Languages: English, basic French

Non smoker

Objective

Why you want to get into yachting and what your future plans are.

Personal Statement

Describe yourself.

What can you bring to a yacht and crew?

Why you would be good for the position?

Qualifications and Experience

List here

Personal Motorboat Experience:

List any boat related experience

Employment History

List previous employers in chronological order with most recent first, with dates when started and finished.

Highlight any transferable skills from previous jobs, use bullet points to keep information succinct and to the point.

This is likely to be the largest section in the CV.

Additional Achievements

Other qualifications or achievements that may be useful in yachting, for example, driving license, massage skills, creative skills like woodwork/painting.

Hobbies and Interests

Anything you do in your spare time for example sports, winter activities, voluntary work.

References

Reference 1:

Name/position

Contact details

Reference 2

Name/position

Contact details

Note: CV should be no more than two pages long.

Acknowledgements:

A big thank you to all my family for all their support during the writing of this article and the hours of proof reading they have given it. Also for the love, support and constant encouragement they have so richly provided through my journey.

To my friends at home who, during my time yachting, it was not as easy to keep in touch with. It was a huge disappointment to miss significant life events and weddings, though you all understood and welcomed me back as though I had never been away.

Also to all the crew and friends I have been fortunate to meet and work with along this incredible journey. To all the Captains who gave me the opportunity to work onboard some fabulous yachts, and finally to the yacht owners who made this whole experience possible.

Work on a Super Yacht

The Beginners Guide

Ben Proctor

Copyright © 2015 Ben Proctor

Amazon Edition

Proof

Made in the USA
Charleston, SC
05 June 2015